'E

D0342624

AVON PUBLIC LIBRARY
BOX 977 / 200 BENCHMARK RD.
AVON, COLORADO 81620

THE MAN WHO STALKED EINSTEIN

B&T 4/15 26.95

THE MAN WHO STALKED EINSTEIN

How Nazi Scientist Philipp Lenard Changed the Course of History

Bruce J. Hillman, Birgit Ertl-Wagner, and Bernd C. Wagner

Guilford, Connecticut

An imprint of Rowman & Littlefield
Distributed by NATIONAL BOOK NETWORK

Copyright © 2015 by Bruce J. Hillman, Birgit Ertl-Wagner, and Bernd C. Wagner

All rights reserved. No part of this book may be reproduced in any form or by any electronic or mechanical means, including information storage and retrieval systems, without written permission from the publisher, except by a reviewer who may quote passages in a review.

British Library Cataloguing in Publication Information Available

Library of Congress Cataloging-in-Publication Data Available
Hillman, Bruce J.
The man who stalked Einstein : how Nazi scientist Philipp Lenard changed the course of history / Bruce J. Hillman, Birgit Ertl-Wagner, and Bernd C. Wagner.
pages cm
Includes bibliographical references and index.
ISBN 978-1-4930-1001-1 (hardcover)
ISBN 978-1-4930-1569-6 (ebook)
1. Lenard, Philipp, 1862–1947. 2. Einstein, Albert, 1879–1955. 3. Relativity (Physics) 4. National socialism and science. 5. Jewish scientists—Germany. I. Ertl-Wagner, Birgit, 1970– II. Wagner, Bernd C., 1968– III. Title.
QC16.L4H55 2015
530.092—dc23

                                                                2014043486

∞ ™ The paper used in this publication meets the minimum requirements of American National Standard for Information Sciences Permanence of Paper for Printed Library Materials, ANSI/NISO Z39.48-1992.

For my wife Pam, who gives me love, encouragement,
and much to think about
—Bruce Hillman

For Sophie, Hannah, and Clara—we love you
—Birgit Ertl-Wagner and Bernd Wagner

CONTENTS

INTRODUCTION

The Man Who Stalked Einstein is the product of a partnership among three individuals—an American Jew born immediately after World War II and a German couple two decades younger, whose generation still lives with the moral opprobrium of Nazi abuses. Friends for over a decade, we approached writing our book from different but complementary perspectives to achieve common goals: We wished to write a history on an important topic. We also wanted to write a good story in an entertaining, creative style that would read like a novel and appeal to a broad audience. Although we narrate when necessary, we had a strong preference for our characters to express themselves in their own words. To the extent the historical record allows, we give vent to their unique voices.

We believe the result is a compelling story that weaves together engaging characters, their dramatic actions, and the tumultuous times in which they lived. In addition, we explain in plain English the research and scientific philosophies of Philipp Lenard, Albert Einstein, and their contemporaries so as to make them approachable to all readers.

There are several reasons why we decided to write this book. Foremost among these is that the antagonistic relationship between Albert Einstein and Philipp Lenard makes for a memorable, character-driven story. Einstein and Lenard were opposites in virtually every way. That both men were brilliant scientists and Nobel laureates with opposing views about what constituted important, believable science made some degree of conflict inevitable. However, the enmity that each felt for the other was based on much more than their science. It was *personal*. Lenard was so consumed by his own narcissism, his envy of Einstein's fame, and his hatred for Jews that he sacrificed the integrity of his science and his personal reputation among the community of scientists on the altar of his personal prejudices.

We follow the convergence of influences and events that turned Lenard from a productive and highly respected scientist to a man consumed by racial hatred and an early supporter of Adolf Hitler and his Nazi Party. We detail the environment that fostered the flowering of *Deutsche Physik*, Lenard's irrational and unsupportable philosophy of Aryan scientific supremacy. The acceptance of *Deutsche Physik* by the highest level of Nazi leadership, underpinned by anti-Semitic laws enacted under the Third Reich, enabled Lenard and his like-minded colleague Johannes Stark to purge Germany's institutes and universities of many of the greatest scientists of the era and force them to immigrate to countries with which Germany would soon be at war.

Oddly enough, the idea for this book had its origins on the lunarlike landscape of the Cruden Bay golf links just north of Aberdeen, Scotland. There, fate paired me for a round of golf with two brothers. Their father had been a Canadian army officer attached to the U.S. military to observe early nuclear weapons testing. Our conversation about what he had told them of his experiences carried us through eighteen holes and a long and bibulous dinner at a nearby pub right up until "last call." Having just completed writing a book on medical imaging for lay audiences, I was looking to do something different. Some aspect of the race to develop an atomic weapon seemed like just the ticket. After a number of false starts, my research led me to the curled yellowed pages of a 1946 medical journal detailing Colonel Lewis E. Etter's postwar interviews of Philipp Lenard. Doctor Etter had recently been discharged from the U.S. Army Medical Corps and would soon return to the United States to complete his training in radiology. Despite all evidence to the contrary, Lenard claimed that he, not Wilhelm Conrad Roentgen, was responsible for discovering X-rays. Researching further, I found that Lenard's conflicts over the delegation of credit for scientific discoveries extended to the British physicist J. J. Thompson, as well as Marie Curie and Albert Einstein. In Lenard's brilliantly self-centered and paranoid character, I saw the makings of a powerful story.

The problem for me, of course, was that many of the letters, writings, and secondary sources that would be essential to writing *The Man Who Stalked Einstein* existed only in German. Translations of Lenard's writings, in particular, would be especially hard to come by. Unable to translate German, I approached Birgit and Bernd with a proposal.

I had known Birgit since 2001, when she had successfully applied for a medical research fellowship in the United States, under my tutelage. I met her husband Bernd just a few months later when they traveled to the United States for a medical meeting. In 2012, over cocktails one evening during a conference in Vienna, Birgit and I worked out the parameters of our partnership: I would research, write, and relate to our agent, editor, and publisher—should we be fortunate enough to find one. Birgit and Bernd would research, translate, edit, and suggest the inclusion of material I had overlooked. Together, we shared a common vision that made writing *The Man Who Stalked Einstein* interesting and fun. We hope you will agree that this book fulfills our hopes for our collaboration.

Bruce Hillman, Birgit Ertl-Wagner, and Bernd Wagner

October 2014

A NOTE ON THE DIFFERENCES BETWEEN LENARD'S AND EINSTEIN'S SCIENCE

The natural sciences took a great leap forward during the period covered by our book, from the late 1800s until the end of World War II, an era in which scientists modeled the atom and began to develop new theories about the workings of the cosmos.

Lenard's experimental physics and Einstein's theoretical physics represent two opposing schools of thought that came into conflict throughout Europe (but most notably in Germany) during the first decades of the twentieth century. Basing their work on classical mechanics derived from the discoveries of such greats as Isaac Newton, Nicolaus Copernicus, and Johannes Kepler, the experimentalists believed that valid new knowledge was the product of "induction." Induction calls for a scientist to express a hypothesis; design experiments to test the correctness of the hypothesis; observe whether the results support or reject the hypothesis; and, in the end, employ proven hypotheses to construct laws describing the behavior of natural phenomena.

In contrast, theoretical physics is primarily based on "deduction," wherein scientists express new understandings of how the universe works based on established knowledge and their assumptions concerning unknown principles. To show the plausibility of his theories, Einstein famously designed "thought experiments" using familiar, everyday phenomena to make his theories relevant and understandable. Even so, his theories awaited experimental observations to ultimately determine their accuracy and utility.

Newton's universal law of gravity provides a classic example of induction. The law states that the gravitational force exerted by an object is proportional to the square of its mass and inversely proportional to the square of the distance between the two masses. In other words, larger objects exert more gravitational pull than smaller objects, and the impact of gravity lessens as the distance between objects grows farther apart. Newton's work on gravity began with observation. Based on his observations, Newton formed a hypothesis about how gravity worked. He then designed a series of experiments that allowed Newton to accept or reject the hypothesis based on his results. By repeating this process for a series of hypotheses, he ultimately arrived at his law of gravitation.

The problem is that while the laws of classical physics hold up well for many applications, they do not quite work for all applications, especially when miniscule masses like atoms and subatomic particles and high velocities are involved. As a generalization, phenomena that do not fall into the realm of human perception are often difficult to interpret using the laws of classical physics. With advances in instrumentation improving the accuracy of quantitation of natural occurrences, breaches in the applicability of Newtonian physics became more evident.

Kepler's law is one example where Einstein's theoretical physics provided a plausible explanation of an exception to a law of classical physics. One part of Kepler's law states that planets orbit the sun in a regular and reproducible ellipse with the sun residing at one of the focal points of the ellipse. However, by Einstein's time, it became evident that there was a small but definite irregularity in the orbit of Mercury that conflicted with Kepler's law. The point of Mercury's orbit when the planet is nearest the sun—known as its "perihelion"—actually changes from orbit to orbit. Calculations based on Einstein's theory of general relativity explained the shifting perihelion. As we detail in this book, Einstein's explanation of the shifting perihelion of Mercury was an important factor in validating the utility of his theory of general relativity.

Another example of how theoretical physics gained acceptance was Einstein's use of the concept of a curved universe to predict that light emitted by stars directionally adjacent to our sun bends under the influence of the sun's gravity. Arthur Eddington's much-ballyhooed experiment, which was conducted during an expedition to Africa and South America to witness the 1919 solar eclipse and is also described in our book, proved Einstein correct. The publicity surrounding the occasion shot Einstein to international celebrity and produced converts to his theories.

An important point of disagreement between experimentalists and theorists was Einstein's unified construct of space and time. First proposed by the eighteenth-century philosopher Immanuel Kant, and fundamental to Einstein's theory of relativity, Einstein held that space and time do not exist in isolation but are dependent on the observer's frame of reference. This idea was alien to the experimentalists who held that space and time were distinct, absolute entities. To help bring home the theorists' point of view, consider the following "thought experiment":

> A train travels along a track. A man inside the train measures the amount of time it takes for a beam of light to travel from the ceiling to the floor of the train and back again. Another man, standing stationary alongside the track as the train passes, makes the same measurement. To the man inside the train, the light beam appears as a vertical shaft. Because the train is moving, the man standing beside the tracks sees the light as a diagonal beam of greater length than the perpendicular. Because the speed of light is invariable, the longer diagonal requires more time to complete its path. Both frames of reference are valid, yet the two yield different results. Hence, the amount of time for the light beam to travel its course is *relative*, depending on the perspective of the observer.

As we describe later in this book, Lenard mocked this critical aspect of the principle of relativity during his 1920 public debate with Einstein, unsuccessfully attempting to egg Einstein into a statement he might regret.

The experimentalists also disputed the theorists' penchant for expressing their deductions in the shorthand of advanced mathematics. Experimental physics required only that a scientist be accomplished at basic mathematical skills and have familiarity with classical Euclidean geometry. In general, the experimental physicists of the early twentieth century relied more on describing observations than expressing mathematical formulae. The experimentalists were deeply suspicious that the theorists' frequent use of advanced mathematics was, at best, to obscure what they'd done, if not to disseminate outright falsehoods. The experimentalists, unable or unwilling to shift to the new paradigm, were ill prepared to participate in the new physics or even to effectively critique the theorists' mathematically derived constructs. Lenard, in particular, grew resentful as Einstein attracted young adherents, who were intrigued by the capabilities of the theoretical approach and more facile than their elders with advanced mathematics.

Finally, Einstein and Lenard clashed over the existence of "ether." Lenard was particularly attached to the notion that the transmission through space of electromagnetic radiation, like light and X-rays, as well as gravitation, depended on a so-called ether. This is ironic because Lenard was an arch-experimentalist. Despite extensive experimentation, neither he nor anyone else had been able to demonstrate the existence of ether since Christiaan Huygens proposed the idea in the seventeenth century. Einstein's theoretical universe disdained ether as requiring a special frame of reference apart from all others with respect to electromagnetism in contradiction of his theory of special relativity. Einstein proposed that quanta of light and other radiant energies were self-sustaining as they moved through space. During the two decades when Lenard stalked Einstein, he repeatedly brought up Einstein's disbelief in ether as though it were a moral failing of religious proportions.

Lenard and Einstein's scientific differences sparked their heated interpersonal dispute that highlighted an era of intellectual tumult and led to the dismantling of the natural sciences in Germany. The resultant international diaspora of German natural scientists, the most accomplished scientific community of its era, still influences the science of today.

I

PYRRHIC VICTORY

Sieg heil!

The man's cry found an echo in a thousand others. On the clear, cool evening of May 11, 1933, the crowd repeated the familiar Nazi greeting as ranks of university students marched past encouraging throngs of spectators into the vast expanse of Berlin's Opera Square. The students arranged themselves around an enormous blaze that the brown shirts of the Nazi SA had set and stoked into an inferno earlier in the evening. Sparks shot into the late spring night, their explosive barks all but drowned out by the cheers of more than forty thousand onlookers.

Young faces reflected the heat of the bonfire and their excitement at having all eyes upon them for this historic moment. At a signal, the front rows of students moved forward, stooped to gather armfuls of books, and tossed them into the flames. They gave way to the students behind them, reciting as they did the prescribed verses each had committed to memory:

> Against class warfare and materialism; for the community of the people and an idealistic way of life!
> Against decadence and moral degeneracy; for decency and custom in family and government!

The ritual was repeated until the flames had consumed twenty-five thousand books. Among the dozens of authors whose writings had been trucked from libraries to Opera Square earlier in the day were socialists like Karl Marx, social activists like Helen Keller, and humanists like Ernest Hemingway. Organizers also had removed from the library stacks every copy they could find of the works of a number of Jewish scientists. Their revolutionary discoveries had helped elevate German science to the apotheosis of world recognition. Under the new Nazi regime, they had fallen out of favor.

As the flames snapped and flexed in the wind, and the logs fueling the blaze settled into embers, a lone figure limped up several steps to a roughly constructed platform fronting the square. The chief of Nazi propaganda, Reichsminister Joseph Goebbels, surveyed his audience. His sweating, lupine face gleamed in the shifting light. When he sensed the crowd's anticipation had grown as taut as it could bear, he began to speak.

> The age of an overly refined Jewish intellectualism has come to an end, and the German revolution has made the road clear again for the German character. In the past fourteen years, comrades, as you have been forced in silent shame to suffer the humiliations of the November Republic, the libraries became filled with trash and filth from Jewish asphalt litterateurs.

He paused to give the crowd space to roar its disapproval.

> You do well, in these midnight hours, to consign the unclean spirit of the past to the flames. . . . The old lies in the flames, but the new will arise from the flame of our own hearts. . . . Let it be an oath to many flames! *Heil* to the Reich and the nation and our leader Adolf Hitler!

Goebbels shot the Nazi straight-arm salute, fingers extended, palm forward, into the cool night air. As the deafening applause settled down, a group of students began to sing the Horst-Wessel song, the anthem of the Nazi Party. The tune was picked up by other students and soon the surrounding thousands. The celebration was just beginning. It would continue long into the night.

One man who did not join in the singing, but who was nonetheless elated with the evening's events, was Philipp Lenard. The 1905 Nobel

Prize recipient for physics, director of the Institute of Physics at the University of Heidelberg, and powerful scientific advisor to Adolf Hitler risked a rare smile. It had taken a very long time, but he could finally gloat about his victory over Albert Einstein. For nearly fifteen years, he had led the opposition that finally forced the relativity Jew to flee his native Germany. The burning of Einstein's foolish scribblings that that evening in Berlin—and numerous other locations throughout the Fatherland—was the beginning of the end of memory for Einstein's outlandish ideas about relativity, of which Lenard had written ". . . even now, were falling apart."

Driven by professional disagreement, intense envy over the public's adoration of Einstein, and virulent anti-Semitism, Lenard had unrelentingly harassed Einstein and publicly denigrated his theory of relativity. Beginning with two dramatic confrontations with Einstein in 1920, Lenard and his minions publicly assailed Einstein as the living personification of an ignoble Jewish spirit in science and a threat to Aryan German culture. He had been the mastermind behind the 1920 anti-Einstein lectures at the auditorium of the Berlin Philharmonic. A month later, he had famously debated Einstein about the theory of relativity at Bad Nauheim. He had too often been forced to stand alone, but he had persevered, was persevering even now that Einstein and his wife Elsa had fled to America. It had not been easy, but that night's triumphant burning of Einstein's work had made it all worthwhile.

It was Lenard and the few who had stood with him who had persistently antagonized Einstein and reversed Einstein's popular standing. By the early 1930s, Einstein had been made to feel like a pariah in the country of his birth. He absented himself from Germany for longer periods than he had in the past, traveling, lecturing on the theory of relativity, and speaking out about German militarism to pacifist groups. Predictably, the end of Einstein's tenure in Germany arrived as Hitler was on the verge of consolidating his power.

In the fall of 1932, as Elsa packed their things for a two-month trip to America, Einstein bravely told friends that they would return to Berlin after he had completed what would be his third professorship in residence at Cal Tech, in Pasadena, California. But he probably knew this was wishful thinking. He found himself increasingly at odds with the rising tide of National Socialism. While Einstein, a nonpracticing Jew who once described his ethnicity as "the son of Jewish parents," still felt most at home in Europe and especially among his friends in the German scientific community, he had no illusions about who Hitler was and what drove his intentions. A few years after leaving Germany, from his safe perch in New Jersey, Einstein wrote about his impressions of Hitler during his run to power:

> Then Hitler appeared, a man with limited intellectual capabilities and unfit for any useful work, full of envy and bitterness, against all whom circumstances had favored over him. . . . In his desperate ambition for power, he discovered that his speeches, confused and pervaded with hate as they were, received wild acclaim from those whose situation and orientation resembled his own. . . . But what really qualified him for leadership was his bitter hatred of everything foreign and, in particular, his loathing of a defenseless minority, the German Jews. Their intellectual sensitivity left him uneasy, and he considered it, with some justification, as un-German. . . . [He propagated] the fraud about the alleged superiority of the "Aryan" or "Nordic" race, a myth invented by the anti-Semites to further their sinister purposes.

In early 1931, Einstein had written a letter of resignation to Max Planck, the elder statesman among German physicists and the man who had recruited him to Berlin. After much consideration, he decided not to send it. Later, in December the same year, he wrote in his diary, "Today I decided to give up my position in Berlin," but once more he did not act on his intention. Just before they left their holiday cottage in Caputh for their December 1932 voyage to America, Einstein said to his wife, "Look at the house very closely. You will never see it again." Elsa took what her husband had said very seriously. She packed thirty pieces of luggage for the brief sabbatical. They would be prepared if the political circumstances worsened.

Einstein's premonitions proved to be well founded. Any hope that he would be able to resume his academic life in Berlin turned to dust as, three months later, the couple prepared for their return from California. On March 10, 1933, the day before they were to depart Pasadena, Elsa's daughter, Margot, was twice cornered in the Einsteins' Berlin apartment by marauding, brown-shirted storm troopers seeking to intimidate her stepfather. The apartment was raided three more times during the next several days. The intruders made off with a number of Einstein's personal items, including a prized violin. Einstein telegraphed Margot that she should make every effort to safely remove his extensive books and papers from the apartment to the French embassy, then leave Germany as soon as she could. She managed to do so and met her husband in Paris. At about the same time, Elsa's other daughter, Ilse, and her husband escaped to the Netherlands. Months later, after he decided to immigrate to the United States, a significant portion of Einstein's papers accompanied him on board ship.

The final insult came during his steamship passage aboard the *Belgenland* back to Europe. Einstein received word that authorities from Potsdam had ransacked their country cottage. The stated reason for the SA invasion was that Einstein was suspected of supplying arms to revolutionary elements. The Nazis confiscated his beloved sailboat—the *Tuemmler*—on the pretext that it could be used to smuggle contraband weapons to socialists. Less than four years earlier, he and Elsa had built their vacation home in the small village of Caputh, only a short drive from downtown Berlin. Both of them dearly loved the rustic beauty and peacefulness so close to the bustle of their daily lives. "For us, this house was a place of comfort and security," he later wrote. "A place in which everyone could find his own happiness and his own content." For Einstein, the ransacking of his cottage was an unmistakable signal that returning to Germany would put their lives at risk. "They'll drag you through the streets by your hair," one friend warned him. When questioned about the Potsdam police searching for hidden weapons in his home, he responded cryptically, "Everyone measures according to his own shoes."

The Einsteins disembarked in Antwerp and sought the assistance of personal friends, King Albert I and his queen, Elizabeth. Elizabeth was a native of Bavaria who had been raised in the small town of Possenhofen, near Munich. The Queen had met Einstein for the first time in 1929, when she invited him to dinner to explain relativity to her. By the end of the evening, Einstein had accompanied her in a duet, playing his violin. Invited to dinner again a year later, "I was greeted with heartwarming cordiality," he wrote Elsa. "These two people are of such a purity and benevolence that it is hardly found." A deep friendship developed between the scientist and the royal couple. Now, Einstein was without a homeland. Albert and Elizabeth took him and Elsa under their sovereign protection.

As he was not yet ready to make up his mind about where he would next live and work, Einstein and Elsa bided their time in a cottage in Le Coq sur Mer. Einstein's residence along the Belgian coast gave him the psychological space to consider his immediate options. Everything would have been perfect except for the rumors reaching them that the Nazi agitator Alfred Leibus had offered a $5,000 reward for Einstein's assassination. Concerned for her esteemed guest, the Queen staffed the cottage with two impressively muscled bodyguards. Whether it was out of fear of these bodyguards or simply that no one wished to risk mounting an attack, Einstein lived there securely.

What Einstein decided to do next indelibly inscribed his name among the Reich's enemies. He resigned his membership in the Prussian Academy. It was an action that he could not have taken lightly. Even prior to the rise of the Nazis, anti-Semitism was rampant among Germany's elite scientists, so his membership in the prestigious society had been hard won. Planck had to campaign vigorously on Einstein's behalf. In fact, he'd even approached Philipp Lenard for his support, unaware of Lenard's growing resentment toward Einstein. Sensing some hesitation, Planck guilelessly asked Lenard if it wasn't appropriate for such a famous theoretician as Einstein to reside in the company of his equally celebrated peers. Lenard famously responded, "Just because a goat may reside in a stable, it does not make him a regal thoroughbred."

In a letter to the Prussian Academy of March 28, 1933, Einstein acknowledged that he owed the Academy his thanks for "the opportunity to devote my time to scientific research, free from all professional obligations. I know how much I am obliged to her. I withdraw reluctantly from this circle also because of the intellectual stimulation and the fine human relationships which I have enjoyed throughout this long period." He cited the "current state of affairs in Germany" as the reason for his resignation and doubtlessly considered the matter concluded.

Unfortunately, it was not. The Academy issued an April 1 press release indicating its members were "shocked to learn from newspaper reports about Albert Einstein's participation in the loathsome anti-German campaign in America and France," scolding Einstein for his "agitatorial behavior abroad." The document went on to note that by withdrawing from the Academy, Einstein also was giving up his Prussian citizenship, which was conditional upon his Academy membership. Indeed, the German government first tried to postpone his relinquishing of his citizenship by invoking a rarely applied tax law requiring Einstein to pay a fine for fleeing the country. Einstein simply ignored the decree, recognizing it as a thinly veiled ruse to bring him back into Germany and arrest him.

The Academy's charge that Einstein had participated in anti-German activities had some basis in fact. Einstein had made a number of statements to U.S. pacifist groups over the previous few months, condemning Nazi antagonism toward Germany's Jews.

Nonetheless, he denied the charges in an indignant letter to the Academy dated April 5, 1933. Although Einstein acknowledged that he had described the German citizenry as suffering from a "psychiatric disease" and that he had urged a "threatened civilization to do their utmost to prevent the further spread of this mass psychosis, which is expressing itself in Germany in such a terrible way," he denied that he had ever been a part of any "loathsome campaign." He stood behind every word he had ever published and asked that, in fairness, his defense of his actions be disseminated to the members of the Academy and the public at large.

The Academy's wrongful accusations had slandered him. He had resigned his Academy membership and his Prussian citizenship because "I do not wish to live in a state in which individuals are not granted equal rights before the law, as well as freedom of speech and instruction."

Having concluded his dispute with the Prussian Academy, Einstein deposited his passport at the German consulate in Brussels and returned his attention to deciding where he would work in the future. Paul Ehrenfest, a Dutch friend, tried to prevail on Einstein to join him in Leiden. Similarly, scientists at Christ Church College in England, where he had spent a number of happy times, argued that Oxford would provide the best environment for continuing his work on what increasingly had been attracting his professional attention: a general field theory that would incorporate all known building blocks of the universe into a coherent whole. While Einstein surely considered these options, he was most taken with the possibility of moving to the United States. During his three trips to the United States, Einstein had been favorably impressed by the freedoms that Americans enjoyed. He also appreciated the absence of a formal class system that in Europe denied advancement to those born into lesser circumstances.

Physicist Robert Milliken had seen the possibility of recruiting Einstein to Pasadena early in their relationship, so the door was open to him at Cal Tech. Einstein might well have chosen this option except for the mistake Milliken made in introducing Einstein to the renowned American educational reformer and secretary of the Rockefeller Foundation, Abraham Flexner. Flexner, who was Jewish, had incited a revolution in American medical education. He had closed down sham medical schools and helped to develop a more rigorous medical curriculum. In the spring of 1932, while visiting Los Angeles, he asked Milliken's permission to meet the vaunted German physicist then serving his second professorship in residence. The two hit it off. They were seen walking together, in deep conversation, late into the evening, well beyond the time Elsa had set aside for her husband and Flexner to meet.

Flexner spoke to Einstein about his plan to start a small, very exclusive research university or think tank. Having secured a $5 million pledge from department store magnate Louis Bamberger, Flexner envisioned a highly vetted, prestigious faculty. It would have visiting scholars but would not present degrees. Although Flexner had decided his institute would be located in Princeton, New Jersey, it would have no formal affiliation with Princeton University.

Einstein had lectured at Princeton University several times and enjoyed the experience. The college's leafy walkways and gothic, fitted-stone architecture were more appealing to Einstein, and especially to Elsa, than the foreign, materialistic feel of Southern California. Sensing triumph, with only one more hurdle to surpass, Flexner timorously asked Einstein what sort of salary he had in mind. The Rockefeller Foundation had given him a generous budget, but perhaps not enough to command the attention of such a great man. Einstein naïvely suggested $3,000 annually, quite a low figure by American standards. Smiling, Flexner told him that he would work out his salary with Elsa. Einstein readily agreed. They settled at $16,000.

The freedom to think and write and the flexibility of the arrangement that Flexner promised so appealed to Einstein that he quickly agreed in principle to become the second faculty member of the institute, after the mathematician Hermann Weyl. This is not to say that Einstein hadn't any qualms about moving to such a strange place as America. He had expressed how he felt about the United States in a 1925 letter to his friend Michael Besso, who had worked with him on the theory of special relativity: "To find Europe delightful, you have to visit the United States. While people have fewer prejudices there, they nevertheless are hollow and uninteresting, much more so than in Europe." In a similarly dismissive vein, he noted, "American men are nothing but the pet dogs of their wives. People seem to be endlessly bored."

The threat to his and his wife's lives demanded that Einstein reconsider those views. In the end, Einstein agreed to spend four or five months annually in Princeton at what would become the Institute for Advanced Studies. In the worst case, he thought, he would make up for U.S. intellectual deficiencies by spending the rest of his time at Oxford or Leiden or Madrid, where he also had accepted a yet-to-be-defined appointment. It was not to be. Despite living another twenty-two years, Einstein never again touched foot on European soil.

Einstein grew restless with domestic life in Le Coq sur Mer while waiting for some signal from Flexner that things were settled with U.S. Immigration and ready for him in Princeton. An unusual opportunity presented itself in the form of an invitation from a wealthy member of the British Parliament, a former army commander and pilot named Oliver Locker-Lampson, whom Einstein had once met at Oxford. Einstein traveled to England without Elsa, who preferred her quiet existence along the Belgian shore.

Locker-Lampson was an admirer of Einstein and was greatly pleased by Einstein's acceptance of his invitation. During the few short weeks of his visit, the two men became good friends. At Einstein's request, Locker-Lampson introduced a bill in Parliament to increase opportunities for Jews to emigrate from Germany to Great Britain. In proposing the law, Locker-Lampson nodded to Einstein, who was standing in the gallery of the House of Commons that day, and said, "Germany has turned out its most glorious citizen. . . . The Huns have stolen his savings, plundered his place of residence, and even taken his violin. . . . How proud this country must be to have offered him shelter."

The shelter Locker-Lampson provided was a cottage on the Norfolk moors. While Elsa prepared in Le Coq sur Mer for their voyage to America, her husband contemplated the universe—or so he said—guarded by two attractive young women who had been introduced to him as Locker-Lampson's "assistants." Einstein happily spent his final days in England drinking beer with his well-proportioned protectors and greeting visitors wishing to meet the famous scientist. The press delighted in photographing Einstein with his shotgun-toting "bodyguards." When asked whether he felt secure with his protectors' sharpshooting talents, he speculated, "The beauty of my bodyguards would disarm a conspirator sooner than their shotguns."

Elsa could not have been pleased with the news of her husband's English idyll, but it is unlikely she was surprised. Married fourteen years, she and Einstein had begun their affair in 1912, when he was still married to his first wife, Mileva Marić. When Marić separated from Einstein in 1914, after he had accepted a professorship in Berlin, he noted, "I am extremely happy with the separation, even though I rarely hear from my boys. The peace and quiet feel enormously good, as does the really nice affair with my cousin."

Three years Einstein's elder, Elsa was his cousin on both sides of his family. The daughter of his mother's sister and of his father's brother, she had been born an Einstein, became a Loewenthal when she married her first husband, and took back the surname Einstein once again when she married Albert in 1919. She and little "Albertle" had played together as children. She was well aware of his wry wit and the devastating effect his intelligence and fame had upon women.

"Marriage is the unsuccessful attempt to make something lasting out of an incident," Einstein once said. Although Elsa usually traveled with her husband and kept a stern eye on him, she soon experienced the same heartache as Mileva had. In 1923, four years into their marriage, Einstein fell in love with his twenty-three-year-old secretary, Betty Neumann. Elsa knew about it, but it was nearly two years before she convinced her husband to break it off. Even so, she could not banish the feelings Einstein had for Neumann. Einstein wrote Neumann, "I will have to look to the stars for what is denied me on earth." Elsa didn't doubt that there had been others. Locker-Lampson's assistants were only a distraction. She would say nothing and focus on her preparations for their imminent departure.

The steamship *Westmoreland* left Antwerp with Elsa aboard in early October 1933. It stopped in Southampton to pick up Einstein and his assistant, Walther Mayer, on October 7, before making its way across the Atlantic to New York. To avoid publicity, Flexner arranged for a tugboat to meet the ship when it cleared customs at Ellis Island. The tug transferred the Einstein party to a car for the short drive to Princeton. For the time being, Einstein was officially a man without a country. He was among the first of roughly two thousand Jewish scientists, mathematicians, and developers of technology—including fourteen Nobel Prize recipients—who would find themselves dismissed from their jobs, unable to support their families, and threatened with deportation to the Nazi death mills that would soon spring up across Europe.

In recalling the many years of strife with his longtime foe, Philipp Lenard cited Einstein as "the most important example of the dangerous influence of the Jewish circles on the study of nature." A month later, any remaining controversy over Einstein's resignation from the Prussian Academy became moot. On the heels of the Third Reich barring Jews teaching in German universities, it also made any person of Jewish descent ineligible for membership in the Academy. Lenard saw his opportunity to further cement his status with the Nazi hierarchy. Noting, "We must recognize that it is unworthy of a German to be the intellectual follower of a Jew," Lenard partnered with his like-minded colleague, Johannes Stark, to vigorously enforce a series of laws calling for the dismissal of Jewish academics from their university employment.

Max Planck tried to head off the carnage by appealing directly to the Fuehrer, Adolf Hitler. It was to no avail. "Our national policies will not be revoked or modified, even for scientists," Hitler told him in no uncertain terms. "If the dismissal of Jewish scientists means the annihilation of German science, then we shall do without science for a few years."

While, in hindsight, Hitler's response to Planck seems maniacally self-destructive, at the time, it was everything that Lenard could have hoped for. In every respect, it must have seemed to Lenard that his victory was complete. Unrecognized at the time were the unintended consequences of Lenard's successful vendetta against Einstein and the Jewish academics. He had unwittingly accomplished something of surpassing significance. Lenard's actions had shifted the world's balance of scientific intellect from Germany to its enemies, most prominently to the United States. Eventually, there would come a reckoning.

2

THE HEART OF THE MATTER

Near the end of his life, Einstein wrote to his good friend Niels Bohr, "Not often in life has a human being caused me such joy by his mere presence as you did." This assertion was a testimony to their more than thirty years of friendly disagreement over the laws that govern particle physics. At times, their conversations grew so contentious that they became completely oblivious to what was going on around them. Famously, on one occasion, they became so engrossed in their conversation that they missed their streetcar stop on the way to a conference. Eventually realizing that they had gone too far, they got off the trolley, crossed the street, and got on the one going the other way. They missed their stop going back as well.

Although they disagreed over specifics, Bohr and Einstein were both convinced that the laws of physics that work for everyday phenomena—those described by Newton and his successors—didn't hold up in the world of atoms and subatomic particles, where things are very small and often move very fast. This was the purview of theoretical physics. The abstruse mathematics of theoretical physics was breaking down the certainties of traditional Newtonian physics, raising questions that the scientific orthodoxy of classically trained natural scientists like Philipp Lenard was ill prepared to address.

Lenard bridled against the new science, refusing to let go of explanations of physical phenomena that were rooted in centuries-old discoveries and unwilling or unable to grasp mathematically derived theories. It was inevitable that Lenard and Einstein would clash over their scientific differences. However, unlike the sincerely inquiring argumentative relationship that Einstein shared with Niels Bohr, what Lenard and Einstein felt toward one another was the very opposite of respectful appreciation: a smoldering, personal cold war that occasionally combusted into a very public conflagration.

Lenard's intense hatred for Einstein went far beyond their disagreement over scientific principles. In the plodding, conservative world of physics, Einstein was a shooting star. The press had gone wild in 1919 with the first experimental proof of Einstein's theory of general relativity. Front-page news stories compared him to Newton, Copernicus, and Kepler, revered names in Lenard's scientific pantheon. While the public adored the witty, unkempt, down-to-earth theorist, who was turning on its ear the long-accepted dictums by which classical physicists explained the functioning of the universe, Lenard was little known beyond the rarified halls of the academy.

How unseemly for such acclaim to be accorded a scientist, Lenard thought. And on what grounds? Mathematical derivations that began in the abstract and were not held to any standard of experimental proof? Complicity with an all-too-willing and gullible press that welcomed Einstein's self-promotion? The frivolous book—*Einstein the Seeker*—that the sycophantic writer Alexander Moszkowski had published with Einstein's full participation? Yes! Yes, to all of these sins and to one more. Einstein was a Jew. He acted like a Jew. Most damning of all, he thought like a Jew. "It was so typical," Lenard wrote, "the unquestionably pure-blooded Jew. . . . His relativity theories attempted to transform and dominate the whole of physics. . . . Apparently, they never were even intended to be true."

Lenard felt that Einstein had unjustly led a charmed life. Einstein had prospered while deserving true Aryans like himself had suffered greatly. The humiliating Treaty of Versailles and the Weimar government's mindless adherence to the repressive terms of the armistice ending World War I had brought nothing but suffering to the German people.

At the same time, Einstein had grown well-to-do on his renown. Since 1914, when Max Planck had recruited him away from Zurich to a professorship at Berlin's Humboldt University and the directorship of the Kaiser Wilhelm Institute for Physics, Einstein had enjoyed special privileges. At Planck's insistence, Einstein had been elected a member of the prestigious Prussian Academy of Sciences and granted German citizenship. Over Lenard's protestations, Sweden's Nobel Academy had awarded Einstein the 1921 Nobel Prize for work so derivative of Lenard's own discoveries and so prosaic as to be better suited for schoolchildren. While Lenard's son Werner had contracted kidney failure and died of wartime deprivation, Einstein's Nobel Prize money was said to have secured the comfort of his two sons, who were living with their mother in Zurich. To top things off, Planck had acceded to Einstein's demand that he have few teaching responsibilities, giving him the time to pursue well-paid opportunities to lecture abroad. It was rumored that Einstein's Dutch friend, Paul Ehrenfest, banked Einstein's honoraria in the Netherlands, safeguarding the moneys from the ravages of the rampant inflation wreaking ruin on the life savings of many German citizens, Lenard among them.

The contrasts between the anti-Semitic, ultra-nationalistic Lenard and the tousled-hair, pacifistic Jew, Einstein, could hardly have been more stark. They were antipodes, complete opposites in their early life experiences, scientific views, and personalities.

Philipp Eduard Anton Lenard was the son of a wine merchant. He grew up in the small Austro-Hungarian city of Pressburg (now Bratislava in Slovakia). From childhood on, he evinced a deep disdain for any learning other than the natural sciences, a bias that only hardened in its intensity as he grew older. Lenard prepared for his career by studying at Europe's major research centers with some of the greatest scientific minds of the 1880s and 1890s—men like Bunsen, Helmholtz, and Hertz. It was an era of discovery based on real-world experiments, and Lenard emerged a dedicated experimentalist. His research into the emanations of high-energy cathode ray tubes earned him the 1905 Nobel Prize for physics and eventually led to him being named professor at the University of Heidelberg. At the same time, however, his upbringing, orthodox training, and conventional life experiences imbued Lenard with a sense of privilege, a feeling of rectitude in his personal dealings that could be challenging for others.

Lenard engaged in a succession of lifelong feuds. His envy of other scientists' fame and his obsessing over "what might have been, if only . . ." led Lenard to make claims of primacy for either himself or his ideological forebears that bore little currency in reality. He squabbled with Marie Curie and the great British scientist, J. J. Thompson, whose pioneering work led to Thompson describing the electron. However, Lenard's most egregious claims involved the discovery of the X-ray. Lenard was among a number of physicists studying the emanations of cathode ray tubes. Almost certainly, he had witnessed phenomena that could have led to his recognizing the existence of X-rays. That he failed to do so before Wilhelm Conrad Roentgen's startling 1895 publication, "On a New Type of Ray," detailing most of what we know today about X-rays, in no way stopped him from insisting that Roentgen was merely a technician who had advantaged himself of Lenard's work and claiming for himself the title "Mother of the X-ray."

Ironically, 1905 was not only the year Lenard was awarded the Nobel Prize but also Einstein's "miracle year." In that year, the previously unknown and relatively untutored Swiss patent clerk published four major articles, including revolutionary dissertations on the photoelectric effect, Brownian motion, the equivalence of mass and energy, and one detailing his theory of special relativity. His mathematically derived insights came like a torrent, spontaneously and seemingly without precedent.

In contrast to Lenard's impressively varied educational pedigree, Einstein attended only Zurich's Swiss Federal Polytechnic University. He floundered in arriving at an acceptable topic for his doctoral thesis, offering several that were rejected by the faculty before passing muster. He finally was granted his doctorate in that same *annus mirabilis* of 1905 for what turned out to be a miscalculation of Avogadro's constant—the number of molecules in a mole of any substance. Off by a factor of almost three in underestimating the constant at 2.2×10^{23}, he later caught his own algebraic errors and published a correction.

Their personalities also were polar opposites. Lenard could be snarky, harsh, and controlling in his dealings with others, and especially unpleasant in how he related to his subordinates. One such relationship involving Lenard and an assistant, Jakob Johann Laub, peripherally involved Einstein early in his career. Laub was an ardent believer in Einstein's work, having written his doctoral thesis on the theory of special relativity. Beginning in 1909, Einstein and Laub conducted a correspondence.

At first, Laub was grateful to be in Lenard's employ, writing Einstein in May 1909, "As Lenard is concerned, he is indeed known everywhere as a satrap, who treats the assistants badly. In my opinion, these people deserve to fall on their bellies. I can only say to them that Lenard strikes an entirely different note with me, and that I have the utmost freedom."

However, by August 1910, it was quite a different story. Einstein's theories contradicted an important aspect of Lenard's scientific ethos, the presence of "ether." Lenard relied on ether as necessary to the flow through space of electromagnetic radiation like light and X-rays. Despite the fact that Laub did not believe in the existence of ether, Lenard required his assistant to conduct extensive but unsuccessful experiments aimed at proving that ether really existed at the expense of his own research. Einstein wrote Laub, "Lenard must, however, in many things, be wound quite askew. His recent lecture on these fanciful ethers appears to me almost infantile. Further, the study he commanded of you . . . borders on the absurd. I am sorry that you must spend your time on such stupidity."

By November, things between Lenard and Laub had degenerated to such an extent that Einstein offered to help Laub find new work. However, even when Laub told Lenard he was seeking other employment and why, Lenard required Laub to continue the ether experiments until he had the promise of a new job. "This is really a twisted fellow, Lenard," Einstein commented after hearing this. "So entirely composed of gall and intrigue. However, you are considerably better off than him. You can go away from him, however, he must do business with the monster until he bites the dust."

In contrast to Lenard, Einstein's eccentric clothing, modest approach-
ability, and gentle wit did nothing to discourage the public's very positive
impression. Einstein's ability to laugh at himself and even his work en-
deared him to people of all castes and stations. He had an absent-minded
air about him that generated innumerable anecdotes. Early in his career,
his first wife, Mileva Marić, suggested that he dress more professionally
at work. "Why should I?" he asked. "Everyone knows me there." She
mentioned it again when he was about to present a lecture at one of his
first major conferences. He responded, "Why should I? No one knows me
there."

Even Einstein's often embattled theory of relativity was fodder for his
humor. As one famous example, in the wake of experimental data supporting his theory of general relativity, he was asked to explain his theory
in simple fashion. Einstein replied, "When you are courting a nice girl, an
hour seems like a second. When you sit on a red-hot cinder, a second
seems like an hour. That's relativity."

On another occasion, when his longtime driver was taking Einstein to
one of his lectures, the driver said to him, "I've heard that lecture so many
times, I could deliver it myself." Einstein took him up on the bet. The
driver did Einstein proud, but afterward, someone in the audience asked a
difficult question. Without missing a beat, the driver pointed to Einstein,
sitting in chauffeur tucker in the back of the room, and said, "That's such
a simple question, I believe my driver could answer it." So he did.

In Lenard's mind, this kind of grandstanding proved his point. Einstein was conducting a referendum on his science in the court of public
opinion. Just because the man could get a laugh didn't mean there was
anything to his theories. In fact, just the opposite. What Einstein was
doing wasn't really science at all. His theories were so abstract. Really,
nothing more than mathematical sophistry. An untrustworthy intellectual
temple built from deduction as flimsy as playing cards. A hoax as cynical
as a street corner game of three-card Monty. Einstein was shilling his
ideas, prostituting himself for the sake of fame and money. Having made
friends with complicit Jewish newspapers and others in the German press,
he had duped a guileless citizenry. That was bad enough. Even worse,

many of Lenard's Aryan colleagues were abandoning their traditional views to line up behind Einstein and relativity. Fueled by a bitter stew of contempt, jealousy, and anti-Semitism, Lenard's attacks became less about Einstein's science than about Einstein himself.

Lenard came to his anti-Semitism by both birth and experience. Though a subliminal hatred of Jews existed throughout eastern Europe in the early twentieth century, it was especially pronounced among the Hungarian nationalists where Lenard spent his childhood and adolescence. Despite being ethnically German, Lenard counted himself among them and was influenced by their zeal. In his adulthood, he shifted his allegiance to Germany, but his chauvinistic fervor never waned. Even so, the young Lenard revealed none of the anti-Semitic passion that so characterized his writings in later life.

Very likely, it was during his educational pilgrimage that he first had negative interactions with Jews that helped lay the groundwork for his prejudice. One of Lenard's professors, the estimable Heinrich Hertz, was, as Lenard described him in his book *Great Men of Science*, "partly of Jewish blood." In fact, Hertz's family had converted to Catholicism, and he had an Aryan mother to whom Lenard attributed Hertz's scientific aptitude. While he and Hertz got along well for the most part, Lenard may have blamed Hertz's frugality for Lenard missing out on an important discovery. Hertz hadn't exactly rejected Lenard's request to buy a better cathode ray tube like the one Wilhelm Roentgen may have been using when he discovered X-rays. Hertz had simply told him to use his best judgment as to whether the cost would be worth it. If only Hertz had given his enthusiastic approval for the new tube, Lenard believed, it would have been he who would have been hailed as the discoverer of X-rays.

Following the armistice of World War I, Lenard incurred a series of financial reversals, which he attributed to Jewish control of international money markets. Already imbued with strongly nationalistic political views and confronted daily with prejudicial Nazi rhetoric, Lenard grew more radical. He fell prey to a popular Nazi shibboleth: the Jews were responsible for Germany's ills. Unlike the masses of ordinary Germans who similarly bought into this lie, many of whom might never have associated with Jews, Lenard not only knew Jews, but also had worked closely with Jewish professors in universities. In fact, he had studied the behavior of one Jew very well. For Lenard, Einstein became "the Jew." He personalized his anti-Semitic views, focusing his vitriol on Albert Einstein.

Lenard espoused that Jews were inherently very different from Aryan Germans in how they thought about science. Science, indeed any endeavor, was subject to unique styles of thinking that were characteristic of different races. In a series of writings formalizing his views with respect to the natural sciences, he touted the superiority of experimentally based German physics and decried theoretical physics as an intentionally fraudulent construct informed by the unwholesome "Jewish spirit." "The Jew conspicuously lacks any understanding of truth beyond a merely superficial agreement with reality, which is independent of human thought," he wrote in the introduction to *Deutsche Physik*, wherein he spelled out the principals that would guide Nazi scientific thought for a generation. "This is in contrast to the Aryan scientist's drive, which is as obstinate as it is serious in its quest for truth."

Lenard doubtlessly believed in the ethos of Aryan supremacy, but to some extent, his rhetoric was calculated to advance his career. As Einstein wrote in 1935, when it came to Hitler's sycophants, "[Hitler's] disjointed personality makes it impossible to know to what degree he might actually have believed in the nonsense which he kept on dispensing [but] those, however, who rallied around him or who came to the surface through the Nazi wave were, for the most part, hardened cynics fully aware of the falsehood of their unscrupulous methods."

Lenard makes a curious assertion at the outset of his autobiography: "My times are not here. . . . The people, as they are around today, probably would not choose to reinvent someone like me." In one sense, this is true. Lenard was a typical outsider throughout his life. He wrote in his *Faelschungs-Buch*, a handwritten account of ideas he believed had been stolen from him,

I was reminded often by my sensation of not having acquired any friend by my work, which was completely unselfish and which was in fact of benefit to many, of which they all have made use with joy. Some, as the sordid [U.S. physicist Robert] Millikan, have acted systematically as robber-knights with Jewish support. Some even have been Jews. . . . I could not possibly be interested in their frankly impossible friendship (which I did not know at the time, but began to sense gradually).

However, in other ways, Philipp Lenard was a man curiously well designed to succeed in his place and time. He was a canny opportunist who capitalized on a political gamble he'd placed on the National Socialists and won. He joined the party well before there was a clear political advantage and was a VIP participant at their 1927 annual convention. He was a true believer who pledged himself to the Nazi Party and Adolf Hitler well before the times demanded it. His demonization of Einstein established his *bona fides* as a man who Hitler could count on to promote his agenda. Lenard's political star rose in concert with Nazi power.

3

FAMILIARITY BREEDS CONTEMPT

Before all the tumult, Einstein and Lenard's relationship had a respectful, even friendly, beginning. In fact, Einstein's first impression of Philipp Lenard was a very positive one. In 1896, at age seventeen, Einstein passed the entry examination for Zurich Polytechnic and began matriculating in the school's four-year course of study for a diploma in teaching math and physics. It was a small program with only six students. One of them was Mileva Marić. Four years Einstein's senior, she was the only woman in the class, among the first to study mathematics and science in Central Europe. Despite the fact that Mileva walked with a pronounced limp and was often in pain, a natural attraction developed between the two students, first as study partners, then as lovers.

During the fall and winter of 1897–1898, perhaps because of her parents' concern that their Serbian daughter was growing too close to the Jewish Einstein, Mileva spent a semester studying physics at the University of Heidelberg. A letter she wrote to Einstein described a lecture she had recently attended:

> It really was too enjoyable in the lecture of Prof. Lenard, yesterday; now he speaks about the kinetic theory of gases. It seems that the molecules of oxygen move with a speed of 400 m/sec., and after calculating and calculating, the good professor set up equations, differentiated, integrated, substituted and finally showed that the molecules in

fact actually do move with this speed but that they only travel the distance of $1/100^{th}$ of a hair's breadth.

It was months before Einstein responded. When he finally wrote, he used the formal German "Sie" in addressing Mileva, rather than the familiar "du" reserved for close friends. He implores Mileva to return, citing a concern for her academic progress rather than any personal interest:

> The desire to write you has finally conquered the guilty conscience I've had about not responding to your letter for such a long time and which has allowed me to avoid your critical eye. But now, even though you are understandably angry with me, you must at least give me credit for not adding to my offense by hiding behind feeble excuses, and for asking you simply and directly for forgiveness and—for an answer as soon as possible.

At the time of Mileva's study abroad, Lenard was serving a temporary associate professorship in Heidelberg, one of a number of itinerant appointments he held while seeking permanent employment. It was during that year at Heidelberg that Lenard decided he had sufficiently advanced in his career and had acquired the financial and social standing he believed necessary for him to take a wife. With all the romance of a banking transaction, he noted in his autobiography that "[I] quickly set up my laboratory and got my experiments going . . . There was an abundance of daughters of professors who were waiting to be married, but it soon became clear how I had to choose." He chose Katharina Schlehner, known as Katty, the stepdaughter of the Egyptologist August Elsenlohr. The marriage would bear two children, Ruth in 1898 and Werner in 1900.

Lenard finally achieved a permanent appointment in 1896 as professor of physics at the University of Kiel, and he became director of its Institute of Physics. By that time, he already had a number of scientific accomplishments to his credit, including his work with cathode ray tubes that six years later would earn him a Nobel Prize. Despite his long academic pilgrimage, Lenard's success was assured. In 1907, his achievements would lead him back to Heidelberg as a professor and director of the Institute of Physics.

There was nothing during his initial one-year appointment at Heidelberg, nor upon his return, that would signal his later animosity toward Einstein. Similarly, he did not betray any overt anti-Semitism. In fact, in his autobiography, Lenard credits the Jewish mathematician Leo Koenigsberger with helping him to cut through the red tape that at first hindered his permanent Heidelberg appointment. "This pure-blooded Jew has always demonstrated more wit and intelligence than most of the Aryan members of the faculty," he wrote, "and since he was smart enough not to want to seem to be of too Jewish a mind, he often was a blessing for me in his cause against the narrow-mindedness and bigotry of the faculty."

At the same time that Lenard was making headway in academia, the much younger Einstein was a complete unknown. He graduated with his teaching diploma in 1900, but Mileva failed her first attempt to pass her final examinations. She failed again in 1901 with a poor score in math. By then, Mileva was three months' pregnant with Einstein's child. She returned to her parents' home in Novi Sad to deliver a girl she named Lieserl. The birth of the child was kept a secret and only became known when a letter written by Einstein at the time was discovered long after his and Mileva's deaths. What became of Lieserl? Had she died as an infant, or was she put up for adoption? Mileva returned to Zurich without her in 1903. She and Einstein married soon after, but despite their having two subsequent children together—Hans Albert in 1904 and Eduard in 1910—the episode with Lieserl, whatever became of her, sowed a seed of permanent discord in their relationship.

In addition to Einstein's marital difficulties, an even more significant problem confronted him. He needed a job to support himself and his wife. Two years following his graduation, the father of a friend helped him get hired into a civil service position after he had unsuccessfully searched for a teaching job. He was appointed a third-class technical expert in the Office for Intellectual Property in Bern, a patent officer charged with judging the originality of electrical and magnetic devices. The position became permanent about the time of his wedding.

Einstein might well have spent a fulfilling life as a patent officer. He enjoyed what he did and was paid nearly twice the amount he could have expected to earn as a newly appointed assistant professor. Moreover, the work was not particularly challenging, so he had time to work on his own thoughts.

And, as it turned out, he was having many thoughts. Indeed, his brain was fairly bursting at the seams waiting for some outlet of expression. While waiting for the patent office job to come through, Einstein organized a small philosophical club he grandiosely named the Olympic Academy. As an undergraduate, he had become bored with the prosaic teaching curriculum and branched off with Mileva into reading science and philosophy. At this time, he returned to those interests along with two like-minded Polytechnic students, Maurice Solovine and Conrad Habicht. The Olympic Academy met regularly, often in Einstein's apartment, to drink schnapps and read Plato, John Stuart Mill, David Hume, and others.

Einstein also scoured physics journals to keep *au courant* and familiarize himself with emerging theoretical concepts in science. Among the publications Einstein read in 1902 and 1903 were Philipp Lenard's investigations of the photoelectric effect. Einstein referenced Lenard when, in 1905, he broached the same subject from the perspective of Max Planck's quantum hypothesis. Einstein derived new insights into the nature of energy emitted when light strikes a metal object. Most gratifying to Lenard, Einstein's publication referenced Lenard's work with the respect the elder man felt befitted his station as an accomplished scientist. Having read the part of Einstein's article that described his experiments as "groundbreaking," Lenard was sufficiently flattered as to have a very positive impression of Einstein.

Suddenly, in 1905, without having given any earlier sign of what he had been doing, Einstein revealed in a letter to his fellow Olympic Academy member, Conrad Habicht, that he had been working on some novel ideas. On first glance, Einstein's reason for writing the letter was to express interest in reading Habicht's doctoral dissertation, but on closer inspection, it is clear that was something of a ruse. The letter is much more about the overwhelming excitement he felt concerning his own frenzy of creativity than his curiosity over what had occupied Habicht. Einstein adopts a self-congratulatory tone in writing this letter to his friend:

> Such a solemn air of silence has descended between us that I almost feel as if I am committing a sacrilege when I break it now with some inconsequential babble. So, what are you up to, you frozen whale, you smoked, dried, canned piece of soul? Why have you still not sent me your dissertation? Don't you know that I am one of the 1.5 fellows who would read it with interest and pleasure, you wretched man? I promise you four papers in return. The first deals with radiation and the energy properties of light and is very revolutionary, as you will see if you send me your work first. The second paper is a determination of the true sizes of atoms. The third proves that bodies on the order of magnitude 1/1000 mm, suspended in liquids, must already perform an observable random motion that is produced by thermal motion. The fourth paper is only a rough draft at this point, and is an electrodynamics of moving bodies which employs a modification of the theory of space and time.

At about the same time as Einstein wrote his letter to Habicht, Lenard sent Einstein an example of his recent work. What precipitated Lenard to send this publication to Einstein? Most likely, Lenard was responding to Einstein's referencing his earlier publication on the photoelectric effect. Einstein wrote back, "Esteemed Professor! I thank you very much for the work you have sent me, which I have studied with the same feeling of admiration as your earlier works." In addition, Einstein commented on the conclusions of Lenard's investigations, which dealt with the generation of spectral lines by atoms at different states of energy.

It was four years before Lenard responded to Einstein's letter, a long enough duration that Einstein may well have forgotten that he had first written to Lenard. Indeed, he probably wondered why Lenard had bothered writing at all. Perhaps, Einstein's growing reputation as a scientist on the rise had piqued Lenard's interest, and he wished to establish contact. Addressing Einstein as "highly esteemed colleague," Lenard began with an apology for having taken so long to reply, then continued,

> Let me thank you for your friendly words on the occasion of my last writing. What could be more exciting for me than when a profound comprehensive thinker finds favor with some points from my work. . . . I am having more and more thoughts about our different opinions on electrical speeds and related things. I think, namely, that we are in some sense both correct; however, I will not be satisfied until I see the comprehensive and prodigious connections found by you to everything remaining, which I imagine fit into the whole picture. . . . With excellent regard, your loyal P. Lenard.

By the time Einstein received Lenard's letter, he had attracted the attention of a number of major academic centers. In 1908, he was appointed a *Privatdozent* at the University of Bern. A year later, he became an associate professor of theoretical physics at the University of Zurich.

Mileva was instrumental in her husband's advancement. She vetted his publications, looked up references, checked his computations, and copied notes, but their romantic relationship had deteriorated. The decline of Einstein's marriage was helped along by the incursion of another woman. A young Basel housewife named Anna Meyer-Schmid had met Einstein a decade earlier at a resort hotel when she was just seventeen. Having read about his academic appointment at Zurich, she contacted him. Einstein sent her a flirtatious letter that included his office address, suggesting she visit him if she got to Zurich. Meyer-Schmid wrote back in kind, but Mileva intercepted the letter and reacted vindictively. She sent Meyer-Schmid's husband a letter claiming that Einstein had been offended by the exchange. Einstein had to intercede. He apologized to Herr Schmid for his wife's jealousy.

Their relationship suffered another blow in 1911, when Einstein accepted an appointment in Prague and then, almost immediately, moved his family back to Switzerland in 1912 for a faculty position at the University of Zurich, where he had done the work for his doctoral degree. While traveling alone to Berlin that year, Einstein reconnected with his recently divorced cousin and childhood playmate, Elsa Lowenthal. Elsa was almost the same age as Mileva but the exact opposite in temperament. Cheerful, bourgeois, and engaging, she was a breath of freedom from the dark moods of his bohemian wife. Upon his return home, he wrote Elsa, "I have to have someone to love, otherwise life is miserable. And this someone is you." He had second thoughts and broke off their secret correspondence for a time, but the romance resumed a year later and took off in 1914 upon his assuming his professorship in Berlin. Immediately upon agreeing to the Berlin appointment, he wrote Elsa, "I already rejoice at the wonderful times we will spend together."

The Meyer-Schmid episode and the new relationship with Elsa were symptomatic of the deep rift that had developed between husband and wife. Einstein's letters tell the sad tale. In 1900, he'd stopped addressing Mileva as "Sie" and moved on to the informal "du." He'd called her endearing nicknames, like "Dollie" and "sweetheart," and written her bits of doggerel like this 1900 quartet:

> Oh my! That Johnnie boy!
> So crazy with desire,
> While thinking of his Dollie,
> His pillow catches fire.

In 1914, after he had begun the affair with his cousin that eventually would lead to his divorce from Mileva and his second marriage, he wrote down his conditions for continuing their cohabitation:

> A. You will see to it (1) that my clothes and linen are kept in order, (2) that I am served three regular meals a day in my room. B. You will renounce all personal relations with me, except when these are required to keep up social appearances. And: You will expect no affection from me. . . . You must leave my bedroom or study at once without protesting when I ask you to.

Mileva's role had regressed from lover to spouse to servant. The cruel tone of this note speaks volumes and reflects a bitterness that went far beyond simple alienation of affection. Einstein may have so wearied of Mileva's company that he could rationalize even cruelty.

For her part, Mileva hated Berlin. In that most Prussian of German cities, she bridled at a rigid caste system that viewed Slavs as being on the same social plane as Jews. She also was much closer than she wanted to be to Einstein's mother, who had a trenchant dislike of her daughter-in-law. Einstein had written to Mileva about the day in 1900 when he had first intimated his seriousness about her to his mother. Things hadn't gone well then, and the relationship between mother- and daughter-in-law had grown worse with time:

> So we arrive home and I go into Mama's room (only the two of us). First I must tell her about the [final] exam, and then she asks me quite innocently, "So what will become of your Dollie now?" "My wife," I said, just as innocently, prepared for the proper scene that immediately followed. Mama threw herself on the bed, buried her head in the pillow, and wept like a child. After regaining her composure, she immediately shifted to a desperate attack. "You are ruining your future and destroying your opportunities. No decent family will have her. If she gets pregnant, you really will be in a mess."

Shortly after their arrival in the German capital, Mileva separated from Einstein and returned to Zurich, taking her sons Hans Albert and Eduard with her. The loss of his children was a severe blow to Einstein. Despite his visiting his sons frequently, Hans Albert, in particular, took his mother's side. It was only over years that Einstein was able to repair the rent in their relationship.

Little did Einstein know that his marriage to Mileva would linger well past their separation. It would cost him five years and a great deal of misery. To overcome his wife's reluctance to agree to a divorce, Einstein made a most unusual contract. Beginning in 1910, he had regularly been nominated for the Nobel Prize in physics. He promised to give Mileva the substantial monetary proceeds of the award should he ever actually receive it. By the terms of the divorce, the money was to be held in trust in a bank. While Mileva would be entitled to draw freely on the interest, she could only use the capital by agreement with Einstein. In the event of her remarriage or death, the money would go to their two sons.

These plans were thrown into disarray by a turn of events. Their younger son, Eduard, was an excellent student. He had begun to study medicine with the goal of becoming a psychiatrist when he took ill at age twenty. He was diagnosed with schizophrenia and intermittently required hospitalization for the condition until he died at age fifty-five. The expense of treating his illness combined with the severe economic inflation that Einstein was experiencing living in Berlin put considerable financial stress on all parties. Mileva struggled with money, particularly during the periods when Eduard was out of the hospital and living at home.

Despite the ongoing marital drama, Einstein's work continued apace. He began to revise his view of Lenard around 1909–1910, influenced by his exchange of letters with Lenard's assistant, Johann Jakob Laub. Laub originally wrote Einstein that he disagreed with the common view around the laboratory that Lenard was a tyrant. Nonetheless, from the very beginning of his employment, Laub's correspondence with Einstein reveals a tension between Lenard's scientific beliefs and his own. Laub's May 1909 letter to Einstein includes the passage, "We have without Lenard a private colloquium in Pockel's [another Heidelberg faculty member] home where we discuss the theory of relativity. In the coming days, we shall proceed to the light quantum theory. . . . I doubtless anticipate your visit. It is not so far to Heidelberg."

The conflict between Lenard and Laub would eventually engage Einstein on Laub's behalf, but not for some time. A letter from Einstein to Laub extolling Lenard crossed Laub's in the mail. "I took great pleasure in this news [of your working with Lenard]," he wrote. "However, I think that the opportunity to work together with Lenard is worth far more than the assistantship and income combined. . . . He is a great master, an inventive thinker!" Despite the compliments, Einstein may have had a premonition of disaster. He concluded with a veiled warning: "Perhaps he will be entirely affable in the face of a man he has learned to respect."

At this point, Einstein's esteem for Lenard was reciprocated. Lenard went so far as to present a paper written by Laub on the theory of special relativity at the June 1909 meeting of the newly formed Heidelberg Academy of Science. The next year, with Lenard's approval, Laub followed up this initial work by writing a paper entitled, "On the Experimental Funda-mentals of the Relativity Principle." The article was included in a volume edited by the man who was to become Lenard's close colleague in his attacks on Einstein, Johannes Stark. Given the symbiotic relationship between Lenard and Stark, Lenard may well have prevailed on Stark to publish his assistant's work. Regardless, the publication makes clear that Lenard was very familiar with what Einstein had been up to, as the work includes a complete listing of Einstein's publications to that time.

Despite the apparent *bonhomie* between the two men, important dif-ferences between Lenard's and Einstein's scientific philosophies were beginning to emerge. In particular, the two men disagreed over quantum theory, of which Einstein was a strong proponent. This was of special significance because Einstein had followed Lenard in investigating the photoelectric effect. Specifically, he employed the concept of energy quanta to develop a new law of physics that would, in time, earn him a Nobel Prize. Einstein's position reflected his willingness to give up on the strictures of classical physics to explain the new phenomena associated with very small particles. In contrast, Lenard held tight to what he knew, preferring to adapt, modify, or expand upon the accepted fundamentals even if very complicated machinations were necessary to make the old ways work. In his 1910 publication, "On Ether and Matter," Lenard was explicit in this regard: "I do not believe the difficulties should keep us from developing and protecting the existing view because otherwise we would discard each such view and even the mechanical comprehensibility of nature."

Even allowing for their differences over quantum theory, their rela-tionship at this time remained cordial. It wasn't long, though, before Lenard's tolerance for the new physics reached its limits. Lenard's regard for Einstein began to deteriorate around the issue of the ether—the mys-terious medium that Lenard believed supported the passage of electro-magnetic radiation through space and was responsible for gravitational effects. Lenard was very attached to the idea of ether, which had held sway for nearly two hundred years. Einstein's theory of special relativity obviated the need for ether, but for Lenard, the abolition of ether from the mainstream construct of how the universe worked was unimaginable. He was prepared to defend ether "even if, in order to make clear the mechanics of the ether, he would have to establish after the ether and its assembly still another ether."

The postulates of theoretical physics had put the believers in ether under the gun to demonstrate its presence. During 1910 and 1911, Lenard designed new experiments based on equations developed by his collaborator, the Norwegian Vilhelm Bjerknes, and set Laub to work. Lenard pushed the disbelieving Laub hard to uncover some expression of ether's presence. It was to no avail. If ether actually existed, it was proving itself a worthy quarry for even as dedicated a hunter as Philipp Lenard. Einstein witnessed the growing tension between Lenard and Laub from afar, his correspondence with the young scientist a window onto the dark side of a man he had admired.

Lenard's disappointment with Laub's failure to prove the existence of ether was palpable. Unwilling to consider the possibility that he might be wrong, Lenard instead blamed the poor outcome of the experiments on Laub. He wrote a letter to Bjerknes in February 1911, which cited Laub's disagreement with the principles of the research he'd been assigned to conduct. "I have arranged these things for Herr Laub with great zeal. He is, however, forever so captivated with the principle of relativity that I always dread that he cannot be correct."

As they had with Einstein, the events of Lenard's personal life intruded upon his absorption with his work. His son, Werner, had been a sickly child and continued to incur health problems into adolescence. His illness excluded Werner from participating in military service during the Great War, a crushing blow for an arch-nationalist like Lenard. Lenard's view of the pathophysiology affecting his son was that he "suffers from the narrow-minded school teaching that ignores the individual and from the bad nutrition during the war." At the same time, his daughter, Ruth, was maturing and had an academic bent. Against the fierce resistance of her father, she secretly qualified for university admittance to study history and languages with the goal of becoming a teacher.

Ultimately, Lenard and Einstein's relationship was doomed not only by their scientific differences but also by their personal ones. Lenard's initial pleasure at Einstein crediting him as an inspiration for his work on the photoelectric effect morphed into a much more negative assessment. Beginning in 1915, with Einstein's first publications related to what would become his theory of general relativity, Einstein broadened his concepts to apply to not only bodies in a steady state, as in his theory of special relativity, but all physical circumstances. He chose as an experimentally provable example of the power of his theory an explanation of the perihelion of the planet Mercury, wherein, contrary to Kepler's law, the point in the orbit of Mercury closest to the sun changes from orbit to orbit.

Einstein's critics went on the attack. In 1917, Ernst Gehrcke, an ardent anti-relativity scientist—and someone who would be linked to Lenard's future efforts to discredit Einstein—republished in the *Annalen der Physik* a 1902 work by a physicist named Paul Gerber. Gerber had devised a formula for explaining the perihelion phenomenon that did not require reference to relativity. Bringing to light the Gerber publication gave Gehrcke the chance to raise the possibility that Einstein had plagiarized Gerber's ideas. He attacked both Einstein's primacy and his integrity in a single blow. It would be the first of a stream of accusations by Einstein's critics—including Lenard's claim that Einstein had cribbed the work of the obscure Austrian physicist, Friedrich Hasenoehrl—that Einstein was fundamentally a plagiarist.

As evidenced by a letter that Lenard wrote to Johannes Stark, then the editor of the omnibus publication *Almanac of Radioactivity and Electronics*, Lenard was in league with Gehrcke: "I would like to ask whether a short original post by me . . . on ether and gravitation . . . could be quickly published in the Almanac," Lenard wrote following Gehrcke's republication of Gerber's article.

Stark responded, "I will gladly include your study on ether and gravitation in my edited almanac. . . . I find it meritorious that you have co-contributed to the acceptance of Gerber's work." In what was certainly a direct reference to Einstein's theory of general relativity, Stark continued,

"The work is physically well thought and is, for me, more likable than so many of the theoretical works, which, with a sort of dialectical sorcery, pretend to solve the difficult physical problems."

Lenard immediately thanked him for agreeing to publish his commentary, which was intended to accomplish several goals: reinforce the rationale for belief in ether; set to right the infringement by Einstein on Gerber's ideas; establish the failings of the theory of general relativity; and, in Lenard's words, make clear that "the ether explanation of gravitation [believed at the time to act as a radiomagnetic wave] . . . appears good to me because it is so simple that by it alone, everything works."

Unfortunately for Lenard, events conspired to put him on the defensive. The very next issue of the *Annalen der Physik* contained scathing reviews of the Gerber article by well-respected astronomers Hugo von Seeliger and a close friend of Einstein's, Max von Laue. Lenard had to choose to either dispute their arguments or withdraw the most serious of his concerns about Einstein. Because, at the time, he was otherwise occupied with scientific and administrative issues related to the Institute, he chose the latter approach and provided Stark with a replacement commentary for the *Almanac*. Interestingly, this revised version was accepting of Einstein's theory of special relativity and even of much of his theory of general relativity. However, Lenard believed that "[t]he principle must give up its universality and no longer claim relativity of all movements but restrict itself to those movements which proceed under the influence of mass proportional forces, as is gravitation."

Given their history of mutual encouragement, Einstein must have wondered about Lenard's assault. He retaliated by publishing in *Naturwissenschaften* "Dialog on the Objections against the Theory of Relativity," a courtly and creative exchange of views pitting the arguments of a hypothetical "Critic" against the defense of a "Relativist." The fictional debate is stylized and civil, beginning with the apologetic tone of the Critic, and directly references Gehrcke's charges of plagiarism:

> **Critic**: So as not to upset you too much, and possibly even make you undertake this business (which you can't avoid anyway) with a certain pleasure, I will say this in comfort. Unlike many of my colleagues, I

am not so full with the status of my guild so as to make me act as a superior being with superhuman insight and certainty (like newspaper journalists about scientific literature, or playwright-critics). . . . Also I have no wish to—as was lately done by one of my colleagues—jump on you like a district-attorney and accuse you of theft of intellectual property, or accuse you of equally dishonorable acts.

There follows an extended interchange between the Critic and the Relativist on such issues as the relationship between very high speeds and the slowing of the passage of time; the different possible perspectives for considering the effects of rapid deceleration; and the perihelion of Mercury. These vignettes afforded Einstein the opportunity to explain certain misconceptions about relativity. In the special world that Einstein creates, the Critic concedes the logic of relativity but with some reservations.

Critic: After your last statements it does seem to me that no self-contradiction of the theory of relativity can be deduced. . . . Indeed, it now seems not unlikely to me that the theory is free from self-contradiction altogether, but it does not in itself mean that the theory should be considered in earnest.

Particularly with regard to the perihelion of Mercury, Einstein argues for the plausibility of his theory rather than its correctness and calls out Lenard's objections:

Relativist: The secular perihelion motion of the planet Mercury had to be clarified. This perihelion motion was certainly noticed by astronomers, and they were unsuccessful in finding an explanation on the basis of the Newtonian theory. . . . In asserting the equality of coordinate systems as a matter of principle it is not said that every coordinate system is equally convenient for examining a certain physical system. . . . However as a matter of principle such a theory of relativity is equally valid as any other.

The Critic is convinced to the extent of the specific examples that Einstein has discussed. However, he cannot help himself. He must ask one more question. At this point, it appears that Einstein is speaking for Lenard as he wishes Lenard might speak:

> **Critic**: After this conversation I have to admit that the refutation of your point of view is not as easy as it seemed to me earlier. I do have more objections up my sleeve. But before pestering you with that I want to think over our present conversation thoroughly. . . . I ask out of pure curiosity: how does the diseased man of theoretical physics fare, the ether, that many of you have declared to be definitely dead?
>
> **Relativist**: If there would be an ether, then in each space-time point there would have to be a particular state of motion, that would have to play a part in optics. There is no such privileged state of motion, as has been taught to us by the special theory of relativity, and that is why there is no ether in the old sense . . . space without matter and without electromagnetic field seems to be characterized as absolutely empty. . . . One can quite well construe this circumstance in such a way that one speaks of an ether, whose state of being is different from point to point. Only one must take care not to attribute to this ether properties similar to properties of matter.

Lenard fought back in 1918, writing a new version of an earlier article, *On the Principle of Relativity, Ether, and Gravitation*, as a free-standing publication. Unlike the compliant hypothetical critic in Einstein's article, Lenard is anything but agreeable. There is a hard edge to his writing. "What Mr. Einstein carried out as 'a relativist' . . . was and is not convincing to me. He touches on certain principal points too little or not at all."

The fundamental difference between the two men is that Einstein made the claim for all reference systems being equally plausible (e.g., his example where the train or the station could serve equally well as the reference point), while Lenard favored using "simple, sound common sense" to favor one reference system over another. This complaint—that the application of Einstein's theory of relativity lacked common sense—would become a long-lasting theme for Lenard and other Einstein critics.

This exchange marked the end of Lenard's and Einstein's discourse until their very public confrontations in Berlin and Bad Nauheim of 1920.

Secular events took precedence. World War I concluded hostilities in November 1918. The Kaiser abdicated, ending centuries of monarchic rule. The weak republic that filled the ensuing vacuum in governance was marked from the start. The Allies' demand for reparations led to rampant unemployment and poverty across Germany. A deadly struggle developed between nationalist right-wing extremists and worker-backed, socialist, and communist interests. The days were filled with angst, anger, and violence, while the nights were devoted to hedonistic gaiety that signaled a sense of there being no tomorrow.

Meanwhile, Einstein persevered. He cemented growing support among natural scientists for his theory of relativity. Measurements made during a 1919 solar eclipse confirmed the accuracy of a prediction of the theory of general relativity, giving new credence to Einstein's theory and making him an unlikely international celebrity. In the same year, soon after his divorce from Mileva was final, he married Elsa. It was to become a marriage of convenience in which both Elsa and Einstein accepted their shares of a tacit bargain.

Elsa lived the life of a spouse of a famous man, reveling in the travel, social status, and comfort her marriage afforded her. Einstein could focus on his work, secure in the knowledge that Elsa would handle the details of his daily life while allowing him the freedom to seek romance in sleeker, more ardent arms. His letters reveal that he took several lovers during his marriage and that, at least on some occasions, he discussed his relationships with Elsa. Writing to Elsa of one paramour, socialite Ethel Michanowski, he noted,

> Mrs. M definitely acted according to the best Christian-Jewish ethics:
> 1) one should do what one enjoys and what won't harm anyone else;
> and 2) one should refrain from doing things one does not take delight
> in and which annoy another person. Because of 1) she came with me,
> and because of 2) she didn't tell you a word. Isn't that irreproachable?

Soon after the end of the war, Lenard further tightened his grip on every aspect of his institute, becoming more remote in his dealings with the students and his subordinates. He mourned the death of his only son.

"He was not given the privilege to take part in the war. . . . With him, the last bearer of my name left the earth." Lenard grew more radical. He became a believer in the widespread but outrageous notion that the German army had not been defeated in battle but had been "stabbed in the back" by the pacifists, republicans, and Jews who had sued for peace. Passages from his autobiography detailing this period provide early evidence of his developing anti-Semitism.

> When the army returned after four years, not defeated in combat, they found a spiritually decimated patrimony. . . . The pseudo-blossoming that was to be observed soon at center stage of the relativity theory and the sudden increase in scientific journals could not have been comprehended if not even uninitiated people had increasingly understood who the real victors of the great war had been: the Jews in their now free unfolding of their own spirit.

In 1920, Lenard was fifty-eight years old, Einstein a comparatively youthful forty-one. Lenard put aside his dispute with Einstein in 1918 to address more immediate concerns, but he didn't forget about it. Their simmering conflict was about to become a very public conflagration.

4

AN INTERESTING EVENING OUT

In his office at the Institute of Physics in Heidelberg, Philipp Lenard lifted his eyes from the August 6, 1920, edition of *Taegliche Rundschau* and smiled. Under the rubric of the Working Society of German Scientists for the Preservation of Pure Science, he and a group of right-minded colleagues had launched the first salvo of their efforts to restore sanity to the physical sciences. The headline jumped from the page: "Einstein's Theory of Relativity—A Scientific Mass Hysteria." The article charged Albert Einstein and his friends in the Berlin press with purposely pursuing a cynical promotional campaign to delude the public with his fraudulent theory of relativity. The byline attributed the article to Paul Weyland, the man Lenard had met with just five days earlier in this very office.

The renowned scientist and acknowledged leader of the movement to debunk relativity had been impressed by Weyland's fiery Aryan spirit, as well as his sincerity in wanting to dispel the public adoration of the "un-German" Einstein. Moreover, his credentials perfectly suited the broader goals of Lenard's plans. Weyland was an outspoken member of the ultranationalist German National People's Party and the editor of the anti-Semitic periodical, *Deutsch-Voelkische Monatshefte*. Although he claimed to have trained as a chemical engineer, he could produce no documentation to this effect and had been making his living as a publicist for some of the shadier elements of Germany's burgeoning radical, right-wing political groups. His detractors claimed that he possessed a special

talent for speaking in half-truths and for arousing the baser passions of .
the common man. Lenard saw in Weyland the perfect cat's paw to attack
Einstein's self-promotion and the growing popularity of his theories. As
he reread the newspaper article, Lenard felt reassured that Weyland was
the right man, one whose conscience would not prove a barrier to pursuing their plan.

Weyland was a man perfectly made for his times. Berlin had changed
greatly in the aftermath of World War I from a grim, gray city of humor-
less Prussian values to one that was game for almost anything. Liberated
from the stultifying mores that had bound them, the citizenry pursued
novelty in science, culture, and the arts. Cafés, cabarets, and erotic night-
clubs stayed open well into the early morning hours.

At the same time, the political atmosphere was tense. Germany had
signed a punitive armistice, the Treaty of Versailles, which demanded the
equivalent of $33 billion in U.S. dollars in reparations. Inflation was
rampant, for many citizens destroying in weeks the savings of a lifetime.
Before the war, the German mark had traded at roughly four to the dollar.
By July 1923, the exchange rate was eighteen thousand marks to buy a
dollar, slipping five months later to 4 billion.

The deprivation spawned a rabid tangle of radical, reactionary political groups that threatened the fragile fiber of the Weimar government. In
1920 alone, nationalistic activists had already fomented considerable dis-
ruption by the time Weyland published his anti-Einstein tirade. An attempted coup by the right-wing Luettwitz–Kapp faction nearly succeeded
in toppling the government. In Goettingen, delegates of the university's
student government proposed expelling Jewish students from all German
universities. "The Jewish question" was further addressed in the platform
of the German Workers Party (or DAP, for Deutsche Arbeiterpartei). In
February, speaking before a deliriously supportive crowd of two thousand
in the main hall of Munich's Hofbraeuhaus, Adolf Hitler detailed the
party's twenty-five-point plan to restore national pride. Among the pro-
posals were the cancellation of the Treaty of Versailles and the withdrawal of German citizenship from the country's Jews, whom he claimed were
responsible for many of Germany's economic ills.

The DAP was new on the scene, having just been founded in 1919 by a metal worker, Anton Drexler, and a journalist, Karl Harrer. It initially boasted twenty-four members, mostly friends of Drexler's from the Munich railway plant. The meetings of the DAP took place in the back rooms of small pubs until the party established offices in another of Munich's beer halls, the Sterneckerbraue, and then the Gasthaus Cornelius. Ironically, Adolf Hitler initially joined the DAP as a government spy. The German army assigned Corporal Hitler, still on active duty following the war, to infiltrate the DAP and inform them of party activities. Hitler got caught up in the politics of the organization and soon became DAP chairman.

In short order, he changed the DAP from a comedic parody of a political fringe party to one that could seriously contend in local elections. Hitler changed the name of the organization to the National Socialist German Workers Party (or NSDAP, for Nationalsozialistische Deutsche Arbeiterpartei), best known as the Nazis. He brought in new young members, the precursors of the SA paramilitary "brown shirts," to guard the meeting hall against the invasion of rival political parties. Order was strictly enforced.

Weyland's Jeremiad against Einstein was directed at members of the general public, many of whom had already been radicalized by Germany's harsh economic conditions. An avowed Jew-baiter who had publicly chided the DAP for being too soft on the "Jewish question," Weyland pandered to the xenophobic paranoia of his audience. He accused Einstein of plagiarizing others' work and concluded that the theory of relativity was nothing more than an "enormous bluff." Without explicitly invoking anti-Semitic language, he nonetheless planted seeds of doubt about whether the Jewish Einstein could be trusted as a true German. He cited in his article a "particular press, a particular community," which he charged with engaging in a pro-Einstein promotional campaign to build public currency for Einstein's theories and popular celebrity for their progenitor. Lenard knew—indeed, everyone who had spent the least amount of time in Berlin understood—that Weyland was referring to the *Berliner Tageblatt*, called by some the *Judenblatt*, or "Jew paper."

In the minds of the Working Society members, the evidence for Weyland's accusations was incontrovertible. There was a widening schism in physics that separated the theorists from the experimentalists. They were not just academic differences but cultural as well. Lenard had been incensed by a recent *Berliner Tageblatt* article that had drawn ridiculous parallels between Einstein's mathematically deduced theories—so characteristic of Jewish science—and the work of immortal Aryan experimentalists like Newton, Copernicus, and Kepler. Waxing eloquent, the author had likened Einstein's theories to "an oracular saying from the depths of the skies." Stirred by this kind of overblown rhetoric, the public mania over Einstein was reaching ridiculous proportions. And Einstein himself was at the bottom of it. It was unworthy of a true scientist to engage in self-promotion.

The day after meeting with Weyland, Lenard wrote his younger colleague, Johannes Stark, to inform him of what had transpired during their conversation. "Mr. Weyland is very enthusiastically in agreement with our plans to halt the un-German influences. He was here with me yesterday. We discussed plans for a Working Society of German scientists to maintain the purity of science. I particularly suggested that he connect with you to be certain that there won't be inefficient duplication of efforts and that no fragmentation adversely affects our plans for Bad Nauheim" (the site of an important annual German scientific conference scheduled for the following month).

The convergence of Lenard's and Weyland's interests set in motion plans for an extended anti-relativity campaign. Weyland's article was only the beginning. The Jew was still riding high, but he would soon experience the changing tide of fickle public sentiment. On August 6, Weyland announced the next phase of their plan. The Working Society would present a series of lectures on relativity. With Lenard's guidance, Weyland had developed a program of twenty public lectures by highly respected scientists, true German experimentalists, who would put the lie to Einstein's mathematical sophistry and false denial of traditional scientific thinking.

Unbeknownst to Lenard, Weyland listed him, as well as several others, as having agreed to deliver a lecture, when, in fact, they had not actually said they would participate. In fact, Lenard had explicitly declined Weyland's invitation. As a prominent scientist, he already was on record as disputing essential elements of Einstein's theories. The appearance of too close a relationship between Weyland—nothing more than a propagandist, really—and himself was not desirable. The risk that the public might associate him with such an unsavory character was unnecessary. He would stay in the background for now. He would come forward when the time was ripe.

To Lenard, Einstein was symbolic of a much bigger problem besetting German academics. His theories were characteristic of how Jews thought about science: all theory, insufficiently backed by experimentation—the backbone of Germanic scientific thought. Relativity was nothing more than mathematical trickery, an untrustworthy intellectual temple as flimsy as the paper on which Einstein scribbled his nonsense. Eventually, Lenard would elaborate at length on his beliefs about the integrity of "Jewish science" in his four-volume work, *Deutsche Physik*. For now, Weyland and Lenard had agreed upon their principal indictment. Einstein had engaged a pandering press to promote his unsupportable theories. It had gotten to the point that, in the popular mind, they were overtaking the Aryan-led natural order.

The near-deification of Einstein rankled to such an extent that Lenard felt it his duty as a true German to rectify the situation. "Then the Jew came and caused an upheaval," he wrote at the time, "with his abolition of the concept of ether, and ridiculously enough, even the oldest authorities followed him. They suddenly felt powerless when confronted with the Jew. This is how the Jewish spirit started to rule over physics."

It wasn't just the general public who had been duped but his scientific colleagues as well. It was time for those natural scientists possessed of the true Aryan spirit to come forward and join together to terminate the Jewish influence. Under his leadership, the Working Society would overthrow this inferior and misanthropic philosophy. The Working Society would restore Aryan science to its rightful place: the supreme manifestation of human intellectual accomplishment.

On August 24, a little more than two weeks after Weyland had published his indictment of Einstein, he stood at the podium on the stage of the 1600-seat auditorium of the Berlin Philharmonic. He and his minions had provided ample public notice of the event. Weyland happily surveyed the hall; his eyes swept upward past the three sections of orchestra seats to the mezzanine, and to the layers of loges. Every seat was filled, and small crowds stood at every available vantage point. Outside the neoclassical, white brick building on Bernburger Street and on the broad steps leading to the main entry, representatives of right-wing organizations plied passersby with booklets emphasizing the danger of Jewish internationalism. In the building's foyer, vendors sold swastika lapel pins and copies of the second edition of a booklet Lenard had written—*On the Principle of Relativity, Ether, and Gravitation*—disputing the theory of general relativity. Literally and figuratively, the stage was set for Weyland to press forward his challenge to Einstein and his work.

"Ladies and gentlemen," he began. "Hardly ever in science has a scientific system been set up with such a display of propaganda as the general principal of relativity, which on closer inspection turns out to be in the greatest need of proof." In this, Weyland was being purposely ingenuous. Einstein's theories were, indeed, based on mathematical deduction. But by 1920, they were not wholly without supporting empirical evidence. Indeed, even the least informed observer attending Weyland's speech would have been well aware of the observations of the British explorer Arthur Eddington.

Eddington had organized scientific expeditions to Brazil and the west coast of Africa to take measurements of phenomena occurring as a result of the 1919 solar eclipse. Foremost among his interests was to assess the correctness of a prediction derived from Einstein's theory of general relativity that the gravitational field of the sun should appear to bend the light emitted by distant stars as it passed close by. Having extensively photographed the position of visible stars positioned near the sun during the brief period of complete solar eclipse, Eddington confirmed a slight but undeniable bending in the range of angulation that Einstein had predicted. Eddington's November 1919 report of his findings to England's Royal Society was the vehicle that had rocketed Einstein to stardom. With Eddington's confirmation, so the media proclaimed, Einstein had overthrown classical physics and established the beginnings of a new scientific world order.

Weyland not only ignored the Eddington findings but also failed to mention general relativity's plausible explanation of a small shift from orbit to orbit of Mercury's closest position to the sun, its perihelion. This allowed him the freedom to skip past the scientific debate, which in any event he was ill equipped to handle, and move on to his true agenda. In a dazzling display of demagoguery, gauged to convince the uninformed, Weyland denounced Einstein as being the mastermind of a pro-relativity publicity campaign orchestrated by a cabal of Jewish newspapers. Through their popularization of Einstein's theory of relativity, they had convinced a guileless public of the verity of a work of fiction.

Albert Einstein was in the auditorium that evening, sitting in a box seat alongside his stepdaughter, Margot. To those around him, he appeared in a jocular mood, sometimes laughing and applauding outrageous indictments. He seemed unruffled even during an uncomfortable fifteen-minute intermission during which Weyland halted his diatribe to encourage attendees to purchase *On the Principle of Relativity, Ether, and Gravitation* at the reduced rate of six marks. Einstein also calmly listened to the succeeding lecture by Ernst Gehrcke, who charged the theory of relativity and its progenitor with having performed "scientific mass hypnosis."

Despite his demeanor, however, Einstein was not unaffected. He was well aware of the rising tide of anti-Semitism. Although there had been no explicit slurs against Jews, he understood that the evening's real agenda was not scientific, but political. The charge that he was "un-German" was code for what was really intended. As perhaps the most prominent Jew in all of Germany, a liberal, an internationalist who had once famously referred to nationalism as "the measles of humanity," and an avowed pacifist and supporter of the Weimar government, he recognized the inevitability of his being targeted by reactionary activists. Nonetheless, the sophistication of planning and organizing the evening's activities, as well as the rancor implicit in Weyland's accusatory tone, must have surprised him.

On August 27, Einstein fought back by publishing a response in the *Berliner Tageblatt* with the ironic title "My Answer to the Anti-Relativistic Corporation, Ltd." First targeting Weyland and Gehrcke as the principal participants in the events at the Philharmonic, he wrote,

> "A motley group has come together to form a company under the pretentious name, the Working Society of German Scientists for the Preservation of Pure Science, with the single purpose of denigrating the theory of relativity, as well as me, as its originator, in the eyes of non-scientists. . . . I am fully aware that both speakers are unworthy of a reply from my pen, for I have good reason to believe that motives other than striving for the truth are at the bottom of this business. . . . I only respond because I have received repeated requests from well-meaning quarters to have my views made known. . . ."
>
> The article further castigated Weyland, ". . . who does not seem to be a specialist at all (Is he a doctor? Engineer? Politician? . . .)," before chiding Gehrcke for his naiveté and accusing him of selecting statements made by Einstein out of context in an effort to make him seem foolish.

Einstein next defended the accuracy of his theories. He named a number of prominent German scientists who he believed fundamentally supported him—the great Max Planck and Arnold Sommerfeld among them—before singling out Philipp Lenard as one of the evening's conspirators. "From among physicists of international repute," he continued, "I can name only Lenard as an outspoken critic of relativity theory."

Perhaps if Einstein had stopped there, much of the unpleasantness to come could have been avoided. However, he could not restrain himself. "Though I admire Lenard as a master of experimental physics," Einstein wrote, ". . . He has yet to accomplish anything in theoretical physics, and his objections to the theory of general relativity are so superficial that I had not deemed it necessary until now to reply to them in detail."

Near the end of his article, he specifically called out Lenard as having been complicit in the events of that evening: "The personal attack launched against me by Mssrs. Gehrcke and Lenard, based on these circumstances, has been generally regarded as unfair by real specialists in the field. I had considered it beneath my dignity to waste a word on it."

Responses to the events of August 1920 were heated on both sides. A letter from Gehrcke, folded around the Einstein rebuttal, welcomed Lenard home to Heidelberg from a holiday in the Black Forest. In the same day's packet had come a letter from Stark revealing what had transpired: "Surely you will have read about the Einstein scandal, which has been replayed recently in Berlin and in the local press. Einstein has thrown out every theoretical achievement of yours and adjudicated in favor of superficiality."

Although Einstein's charge of complicity in the evening's events was true enough, Lenard very much resented being accused of involvement when he painstakingly had sought to conceal his role. In a September 8 letter to Stark, Lenard wrote,

> I am astonished by this personal element that Mr. Einstein and Mr. von Laue [a friend of Einstein and a 1914 Nobel Laureate who also published a critique of the Philharmonic events] hold in the matter and that they believe that they can turn against me. . . . My purely factual objections are to refute the generalized theory of relativity so that Einstein must precisely demonstrate it, instead of being naughty. . . . In short, I do not have the slightest desire to be in the company of Einstein unless. . . . I am a part of the whole that either passes or fails [his theories].

Beginning shortly after the time Lenard became aware of Einstein's newspaper speculations on his role in the Berlin Philharmonic episode, he became even more hostile toward Einstein, and his words and writings more openly anti-Semitic. What had been primarily a conflict of scientific positions had transformed into something pointedly personal.

Among the pro-Einstein faction, there was concern that Einstein had incautiously let his emotions get the better of him, charging Lenard with actions he could not substantiate. Many of his friends and admirers worried that, out of either fear for his safety or a feeling of being unappreciated, Einstein might emigrate to any number of countries that would welcome him with open arms. It was common knowledge that Einstein's friend, Paul Ehrenfest of the University of Leiden in the Netherlands, was particularly interested in bringing Einstein to Holland and had offered the likelihood of a professorship. Few doubted that there would be other bidders should Einstein express an interest in emigrating.

It had been no easy matter six years previous to recruit Einstein to Berlin from his professorship in Zurich, where he had landed after a brief tenure at the Charles-Ferdinand University in Prague. Einstein's star was rising on a meteoric trajectory. He had demanded and received unheard-of considerations to immigrate to Germany—the directorship of the Kaiser Wilhelm Institute of Physics, professorship at Humboldt University, and agreement that he would have only minimal teaching obligations. Now those who had invested so much in his recruitment feared the undoing of their efforts. Why, they wondered, should he put up with such grief when he had so many other choices?

Despite the growing anti-Jewish sentiment in Berlin, Einstein probably did not seriously consider leaving Germany at this time. However, this fact may not have been apparent to his contemporaries. In an open letter to a number of Berlin newspapers, Max von Laue, Heinrich Rubens, and Walther Nernst implored him to continue in his current posts. Nobel laureate Max Planck, and president of the German Physical Society Arnold Sommerfeld, wrote personal letters emphasizing their support for Einstein's continued presence in the capital. Sommerfeld, in particular, made an effort at reconciliation between the two scientists as a way of heading off open conflict at the upcoming Bad Nauheim meeting, to which Lenard had alluded in his August 2 letter to Stark.

Sommerfeld was encouraged that a truce might be enacted when Einstein's friend, physicist Max Born, shared a letter he had received from Einstein. The letter acknowledged, "Everyone needs to offer up his sacrifice at the altar of stupidity . . . and I did so in my article." Sommerfeld asked Einstein to write a letter of apology to Lenard and to recant his accusations publicly if Lenard requested it. In return, he promised that he would ask Friedrich von Mueller, the chairman of the Bad Nauheim meeting, to feature as part of his opening address a warning against the kind of polemics in which Weyland had engaged. At the same time, Sommerfeld wrote a letter to Lenard informing him of the request he had made of Einstein.

However, any hope of civility between the two scientists became moot when Lenard wrote back,

> The thought of an apology by Mr. Einstein to me, moreover the assumption of a suitable response to him on my part, to remain satisfactory, I must refuse with indignation. The comments by Mr. Einstein represent the characteristics which must belittle me in the eyes of the reader. They are a sign of personal contempt for me by Mr. Einstein, whose transformation into the required esteem based on some assurance by me would be very astonishing.

In his stilted, overly formal style, Lenard revealed the stress imposed upon him over what he doubtlessly viewed as a public humiliation. Despite the fact that he actually did conspire with Weyland and others in organizing the evening's events, he apparently felt that Einstein had unfairly singled him out:

> Mr. Einstein finds his words shameful and probably incorrect, as he has publicly withdrawn his statements. Otherwise he could not make up the wrong done to me to the extent that is even possible. The public release of such value judgments about a colleague, such as those made by Einstein . . . is, in my feeling, an improper arrogance and reveals an all time low of nobleness.

Despite Lenard's harsh assessment of his character and the failure of Sommerfeld's efforts to negotiate a détente, Einstein privately celebrated what seemed to him a settling down of the uproar surrounding a series of unfortunate events. The embarrassing episode had passed, and with it the worry it had caused. The promised twenty lectures at the Berlin Philharmonic were aborted after the second installment, a lackluster and poorly

attended presentation by the engineer, Ludwig Glaser. The other scheduled lecturer for the evening failed to appear. Weyland, a potentially
dangerous antagonist, had lost face with his former allies. Gehrcke wrote
to Lenard that Weyland was simply "one of the many dubious types that
had been generated by the revolutionary, warlike city." Lenard responded, "Weyland, unfortunately, has proven to be a fraud."

Reassured by the outpouring of support by his German colleagues and
the retrenchment of the Working Society, it must have seemed to Einstein
that the storm had passed. Einstein exulted to friends that perhaps the
Working Society did not have the following it claimed. As it turned out,
Einstein reckoned wrong. There was much more to come. What he took
for fair weather was actually the eye of the storm.

5

A DISAGREEMENT
BETWEEN GENTLEMEN

Less than a month after the Working Group lectures at the Berlin Philharmonic, on the morning of September 19, 1920, the eighty-sixth meeting of the German Society of Natural Scientists and Physicians kicked off an ambitious, weeklong schedule of more than three hundred sessions. Held jointly with the meetings of the German Mathematical Society, the German Physical Society, and the Society of Technical Physics, a late change in venue to Bad Nauheim had presented logistical challenges. Violent political unrest, rampant at the time in the original choice of Frankfurt am Main, convinced the organizers to distance their conference to a more bucolic setting where unsavory elements were less likely to infringe on the business of science.

Bad Nauheim was a very attractive alternative. The small spa town lies at the edge of the Taunus Mountains, only thirty-five kilometers from Frankfurt. Famous for its carbon dioxide–infused effervescent baths, sworn to be effective in treating heart and nervous conditions, patrons had enjoyed the restorative powers of the town's briny waters for centuries. The red-roofed, "new baroque"–style main building, named the Sprudelhof, and eight similarly designed bath houses had been commissioned by the Grand Duke Ernst Ludwig of Hessen and by Rhine in 1904. Completed in 1912, the interiors were an art nouveau marvel of sea-themed, ornamental detail, featuring marine creatures, water nymphs, mermaids, and ocean waves. Numerous fountains and outdoor pools graced extensive parklike grounds. In sum, the facilities promised a positive environment that offered both sufficient space for formal events and informality conducive to more intimate conversation.

Because the conference was the first major scientific meeting in Germany after the end of the war, interest was even greater than usual. As retribution for the war, German scientists were excluded from participation in scientific congresses throughout the rest of Europe. Many were concerned that their isolation disadvantaged them in the competition that exists at the highest levels of science. These fears doubtlessly contributed to the strong turnout of more than 2600 scientists. Those attending knew that the eyes of the scientific world would be watching.

In the audience for Chairman Mueller's opening address were seventeen physicists, chemists, and mathematicians who already had been awarded or would eventually receive a Nobel Prize for their innovative research. Among them were Philipp Lenard and Johannes Stark, who applauded vigorously as the chair gave scant nod to his promise of condemning demagoguery before exhorting the gathered scientists to prove their German patriotism in word and deed. As the session progressed, a series of speakers followed suit. The tone of the conference was going Lenard's way. It was time for him to step from the shadows and strike a second blow against the theory of relativity—one that he had reason to hope would make a large impact on the direction that German science might take in the future.

For some time, Einstein had been proposing to the organizers of the conference that there be a session devoted to a general discussion of his theory of relativity. In the passion of the moment following the Berlin Philharmonic lectures, he raised the stakes by proposing a debate with his antagonists in open session: "Anyone willing to confront a professional forum can present his objections [to the theory of relativity] there." The assembled academics expected Lenard and his supporters to take Einstein up on his challenge. As Lenard's objections to relativity were well known, the expectations were that the critics of relativity would base their arguments on several frequently stated concerns, namely that the theory of relativity:

- Was mathematically deduced but did not actually exist in the physical realm.
- Was supported by only scant experimental evidence; what evidence did exist was explainable by error in observer measurements.
- Rejected the idea of there being an ether to explain how electromagnetic radiation, like light and X-rays, were propagated through space; the theory of relativity did not sufficiently address the mechanism of how this occurred to replace what its detractors claimed had worked well for centuries.
- Contradicted conventional notions of space and time; these conventions, dependent on Euclidian geometry, had served science well and should not be replaced by relativistic artifices.

Moreover, Lenard intended to introduce a new wrinkle to these long-standing critiques. Specifically, given the abstract nature of the theory of relativity and the absence of supporting physical evidence, at Bad Nauheim and for years afterward, he would attack Einstein's ideas on the grounds that they went against the principle of "sound common sense." In Lenard's mind, they lacked believability.

Sessions featuring presentations on relativity occurring on September 23 and early in the morning on September 24 set the stage for the open discussion that would conclude the conference. Following the lectures on relativity of September 24, a single door opened to Bath House number 8, guarded on one side by a burly member of the German Mathematical Society and on the other by one from the German Physical Society. The members of these societies were given preferential admission. In all, six hundred scientists jammed into the capacious, richly decorated bath house waiting room; proceeded into the *Schmuckhof*, a monastery-like ornamental court; and lined the gallery. Afterward, what space remained was opened to a waiting line of members of the press and interested onlookers. Paul Weyland was among them. The crowd was restive; a softly murmured expectancy hung in the air. There was the expectation there would be blood.

In such a charged atmosphere, it was a given that only one man could chair the session. Although Max Planck was generally known to be a supporter of Einstein, he had expressed concerns of his own on the subject of relativity. Most importantly, his gentility and sense of fairness were widely respected. On this occasion, the courtly physicist responsible for quantum theory appeared to onlookers to be unusually agitated. Planck had encouraged Einstein to stay in Germany in the face of Einstein's mounting concerns about the bellicose posturing of extremist elements. So far, Einstein had stayed put, but Planck worried that events occurring during the session might cause Einstein to reconsider emigration.

As it turned out, Planck need not have worried. Writing well after the debate, Einstein made it clear that he had no intention to abandon Germany at this time, noting, "It also would be an injurious act when in this time of stress and humiliation I would turn my back on Germany, given the great kindness that I have constantly experienced from the side of my German colleagues and authorities." He concluded, "I therefore consider it my duty to endure in my position until outside circumstances render it practically impossible."

However, Planck was not privy to these sentiments as he prepared to open the session at Bad Nauheim. His major concern was Lenard, who it was rumored would take the lead among the reactionaries wishing to discredit Einstein. The intense dislike of Einstein and Lenard for one another now embroiled Planck and pushed him into the unwanted role of mediator.

In principle, the session was to provide a forum for an open discussion of Einstein's theories. However, it quickly devolved into a *mano y mano* confrontation between Lenard and Einstein. Although the tone was academic, and only intellectual blows were exchanged, it was apparent to all that the combatants were bitter foes who each bore a serious grudge against the other.

Lenard soon got to his main points of disagreement with Einstein. Einstein's work disdained the conventional explanation of ether as the medium of transit for electromagnetic radiation and the supportive element for gravitation. Lenard was not alone. Scientific conservatives frequently expressed concern over the abandonment of ether, despite the fact that two centuries of experimentation had failed to yield any indication of ether's mass or energy.

Lenard also disagreed with Einstein's extension of the principle of relativity to all movements in space rather than just those in steady state. Lenard had earlier written that the theory of general relativity "must give up its universality and no longer claim the 'relativity of all movements' but restrict itself to those movements which proceed under the influence of mass proportional forces, such as gravitation." Indeed, it was over the specific issue of gravitation that Lenard grew exercised.

As reported in the journal *Physikalische Zeitschrift*, the exchange between the two physicists swung from the serious to the contemptuous to outright mocking.

Lenard: I was delighted to have heard talks on the theory of gravitation through the ether today. I have to admit, however, that the simple mind of a natural scientist resents the theory [of relativity] as soon as one goes from gravitational theory to forces other than the mass proportional ones. I relate the example of a braking train. To make the relativity principal work, you add gravitational fields in the absence of mass proportional forces. I would first like to ask you, why is it that it is not differentiable whether the train itself brakes or the world around it slows down?

Einstein: It is certain that we observe effects relative to the train, and we could interpret these as forces of inertia. The relativity theory could just as well interpret these as effects of the gravitational field. . . . You are convinced that this is the invention of the relativity theory people. However, this is no invention as it fulfills the same differential laws of physics as the effects of masses that we are used to understanding. It is correct that some parts of the solution remain arbitrary when one only looks at a limited scope of the world. I would like to briefly summarize that this field was not arbitrarily invented since it fulfills the general differential equations and since it can be deduced from the effects of all masses.

Lenard: Mr. Einstein's explanations did not reveal anything new to me. I am convinced that the gravitational fields that are added need to correspond to occurrences and that these experiences have not been experienced or observed.

Einstein: I would like to emphasize that what mankind considers clear or apparently valid has changed. The perspective on clarity and apparent validity is somewhat a function of time. I am convinced that physics should be conceptual rather than just apparently valid.

Lenard: I have summarized my views in my printed publication, *Relativity Theory, Ether, and Gravitation*. I understand the usefulness of the relativity principle so long as it is only used with respect to gravitational forces. I view it as invalid when all forces are not proportional to mass.

Einstein: It is in the nature of things that the validity of the relativity principle can only be postulated if it is valid for all laws of nature.

Lenard: Only when you invent additional fields.

What became known in scientific circles as the "Einsteindebatte" continued in this vein for some time, surely appearing to many in the audience as though two infants were bickering over a favorite toy. In the end, each man bore even greater resentment for his interlocutor than had been the case before the session began. There was no resolution, no tidy tying up of loose ends, no common ground to promote a better understanding of the utility of Einstein's theories. Sensing the bad feelings, a number of physicists, including Einstein's friends Walther Nernst and Max von Laue, tried to comfort Lenard. Von Laue made an effort at humor, exclaiming, "Einstein, after all, is only a child!" To which Lenard responded, "Children do not write in the *Berliner Tageblatt*."

As the crowd dispersed, Einstein attempted to speak with Lenard in the cloakroom. Lenard would have none of it, saying, "It is now too late," while brusquely brushing off Einstein's advance and leaving quickly. Gehrcke chased after him but arrived at the train station platform too late. He reported seeing Einstein through one of the departing train's windows. There was no sign of Lenard.

Who knows what Einstein might have intended to say to Lenard following their intense public exchange? Had Lenard been willing to listen, what outcomes, if any, might have changed for both of them? Perhaps, none at all. Scientifically speaking, both Lenard and Einstein were set in their beliefs. But perhaps the bad personal feelings between the two could have been assuaged to some extent, and the distant repercussions might not have been so severe.

The confrontation imparted to Einstein a new resolve never again to allow his opponents to upset him so thoroughly. "I absolutely cannot understand," he wrote, "that because of bad company I could lose myself in such deep humorlessness." A few weeks later, Einstein made light of the Bad Nauheim episode in a letter to Paul Ehrenfest: "At Bad Nauheim, there was a cockfight, of sorts, about relativity. Lenard, in particular, figured as my opponent. To my knowledge, it didn't come to any kind of manifestations of the sort you expected."

By the phrase "any kind of manifestations of the sort you expected," Einstein was specifically referencing anti-Semitism. However, that neither Einstein nor the lay press nor the *Physikalische Zeitschrift*, which covered the proceedings, made any reference to racist remarks does not mean that Lenard was free of prejudicial thinking. Lenard's involvement in right-wing, nationalistic organizations, where such rhetoric was common, was already far advanced. Much later, in 1938, Lenard recalled his considerations during the Einsteindebatte:

> I treated and judged the Jew as a proper Aryan person in this discussion according to the view of the time, and that was wrong. . . . It would not have been of use at the meeting of professors [to point out

the flaws in Jewish thinking about science] because the men are also today still blind. Planck had presided over the discussion, which was preceded by three tedious presentations in favor of Einstein.

Lenard retreated to lick his wounds. He wrote of his sense of hurt and isolation in his perception that the majority of scientists in attendance had sided with Einstein. "The abolition of the ether is again proclaimed as a result of Nauheim. . . . Not one has laughed at this. I don't know whether it would have been different had the abolition of air been proclaimed." Among Lenard's keepsakes commemorating the event was a clipping from the weekly newspaper *Die Umschau*, which focused on science and technology. An article attributed to a Mr. W. Weyl, by whose name Lenard had written the word "Jew," reads, "One simply has to state, that Lenard has not understood the very meaning of the Einsteinian doctrine. Consequently, the adversaries did not find each other. The fight remained a fake fight without result."

Despite what Lenard saw as an abandonment by many of his Aryan colleagues, the encounter with Einstein bolstered his resolve to persevere in his efforts to expose the fallacious nature of Einstein's ideas. Lenard wrote, "My letters of this summer have brought together twelve gentlemen who are German enough to tackle the project to turn the miserable Berlin Institute of Physics [meaning Berlin's Kaiser Wilhelm Institute of Physics where Einstein was the director] into a German Institute of Physics." Lenard's meaning was clear. The academic facility that employed, housed, and protected the hated Einstein had adopted an un-German attitude. That would have to change. Among the twelve scientists listed by Lenard were Johannes Stark, to whom Lenard would eventually pass the mantle of *Deutsche Physik*; Wilhelm Wien; and the spectroscopist Gehrcke, who had followed Weyland on stage at the Philharmonic.

The "twelve gentlemen" had met during the conference and agreed that Einstein must be forced to revoke the statements he had made in the *Berliner Tageblatt*, which had been extremely insulting. They intended to press their case in public. They would embarrass Einstein in one of two ways: either by extracting a suitable apology or showing that his failure to acknowledge his error proved he lacked the breeding and nobility of the true German scientist.

What Einstein did next threw Lenard's plans into disarray. On September 25, just a day after the session at Bad Nauheim, he issued an apology, of sorts, in the *Berliner Tageblatt*, the same despised "Jew paper" in which he had published his notorious "My Response." The apology was by proxy, authored by Max Planck and Franz Himstedt, a well-known physicist from the University of Freiburg. Briefly, Planck recounted the conditions leading up to the stresses Einstein had experienced at the Philharmonic. A misunderstanding caused by Weyland's remarks had led Einstein to lash out at Lenard, whom he erroneously believed to have been involved. The brief article continued, "Through the occasion of the recent meeting of sciences in Bad Nauheim, we have found that Mr. Lenard was put on the list of speakers [at the Philharmonic] without his will. Due to this fact, Mr. Einstein has authorized us to express his active regret that he directed his accusations in his article against his highly valued colleague, Mr. Lenard."

Far from satisfying Lenard, the brief statement issued not by Einstein, himself, but by others on his behalf, only inflamed his resentment. The business with Einstein wasn't over. He would bide his time. There would be other opportunities.

As it turned out, Einstein would provide some of the fodder for Lenard's further attacks on his character. Two years earlier, in 1918, Einstein had suffered liver disease, manifested as gallstones and jaundice. A general deterioration of his health kept him bedridden for several months. Among his many visitors during his recovery was the well-known author and satirist, Alexander Moszkowski. Moszkowski convinced Einstein to collaborate with him in writing a book explaining his theory of relativity in simple language for a lay audience. Moszkowski was completing the finishing touches on *Conversations with Einstein* at the same time as Lenard and his minions were unleashing their barrage of criticism over Einstein's self-promotion in the lay press.

At the insistent urging of his friends—among them, physicist Max Born and his playwright wife, Hedwig—Einstein considered the repercussions of his collaboration in publishing the book. The Borns worried that the widespread popular exposure the book might receive would give credence to Einstein's critics' claims that he much too often tooted his own horn. As the Borns were Jewish, they may also have worried on their own behalf that publication of the Moszkowski book might further arouse already rampant anti-Jewish sentiments.

In October 1920, Hedi Born wrote to Einstein,

> You must withdraw the permission given to Moszkowski to publish the book Conversations with Einstein, and to be precise, immediately and by registered mail. Nor should it be allowed to appear abroad either. . . . That man doesn't have the slightest inkling about the essence of your character. . . . If he understood, or even had a glimmer of respect and love for you, he would neither have written this book nor wrung this permission out of your good nature. [If you allow this book to be published], you will be quoted everywhere, your own jokes will be smirkingly flung back at you . . . couplets will be written, an entirely new, awful smear campaign will be let loose, not just in Germany, no, everywhere, and your revulsion of it will choke you. . . . If I did not know you, I would definitely believe it was vanity. For everyone, except for about four or five of your friends, this book would constitute your moral death sentence.

Persuaded that publication of *Conversations with Einstein* might be injurious at a time when seeking public adulation was considered a personal failing, Einstein withdrew his permission. Initially, Moszkowski agreed to halt publication, but the publisher overruled him. Money had been invested. It was too late to stop what was already well under way. With the publisher's permission, Moszkowski and Einstein settled on cosmetic changes in an effort to distance Einstein from the book's contents. The book was published with a new, more neutral title, *Einstein the Seeker*, and a foreword stating that Einstein had not read its contents. In addition, Moszkowski and the publisher deleted much of the material directly attributed to Einstein.

Einstein wrote the Borns a letter minimizing what he believed would be the consequences of the 1921 publication of *Einstein the Seeker*:

> The whole business is a matter of indifference to me, along with the clamor and opinion of all persons. . . . By the way, M. [Moszkowski] really is preferable to me than Lenard and Wien. For the latter cause problems for the love of making a stink, and the former only in order to earn money (which really is more reasonable and better). I shall live through all that awaits me like an uninvolved spectator.

In Heidelberg, Lenard reflected upon the recent events. He would be neither "uninvolved" nor a "spectator." The Moszkowski affair was further proof of the Working Society's accusations. There was no doubting the Jew's complicity. Nearly a year had passed since Einstein had publicly insulted him. He had not forgotten. Einstein remained unrepentant. Sitting in his office at the University of Heidelberg, Lenard pondered his next moves. In time, he would know what to do. After all, he had dealt with a similar situation before.

6

A MISSED OPPORTUNITY

Long before the attack on Einstein at the Berlin Philharmonic and the debate at Bad Nauheim, Lenard had focused his rancor on Wilhelm Conrad Roentgen, the discoverer of X-rays. The conflict between the two men was based on many of the same elements as Lenard's feud with Einstein, and it occurred for many of the same reasons. In Roentgen's case, his serendipitous instant of discovery earned him a lifetime of Lenard's envy.

Lenard had begun working with cathode ray tubes by 1893, when he joined the Karlsruhe laboratory of the famous German physicist, Heinrich Hertz. "Cathode rays are a phenomenon which occurs when electricity is discharged in a rarefied gas," Lenard explained.

> If an electric current is led through a glass tube containing rarefied gas, certain radiation phenomena appear both in the gas and around the metal wires, or poles, through which the current is carried. These phenomena change in form and nature if the gas is rarefied even further . . . rays are emitted from the negative pole, called the "cathode," which are invisible to the naked eye but which can be observed through certain peculiar effects.

By 1894, when he was completing his scientific apprenticeship, Lenard had achieved a great deal, including improving upon the design of early cathode ray tubes developed by Hittorf and Crookes. Lenard's innovation was to employ a thin plate of aluminum over an opening at the cathode end of the tube. This modification allowed Lenard to prove the existence of cathode rays outside the confines of the tube. The opening also made it easier than with earlier models to observe the properties of the rays. The self-named "Lenard tube" and Lenard's investigations brought considerable recognition to the young scientist; after having served in a series of temporary positions for nearly a decade, he was offered a professorship at Breslau in 1894. The next year, he moved to Aachen; during his tenure there, events conspired to embitter Lenard over a major missed opportunity.

On the night of November 8, 1895, while others slept soundly in the university town of Wuerzburg, Germany, Wilhelm Conrad Roentgen made a revolutionary discovery. Working in the laboratory below his living quarters, Roentgen set up his tube and prepared to continue a series of experiments on the properties of cathode rays. Roentgen was working that evening in Wuerzburg not because he was particularly industrious— although his subsequent actions show that he was—but because the outcomes of his investigations were best seen in total darkness. To maximize his chances of a successful evening of experimentation, Roentgen tightly drew heavy drapes over the windows and locked his laboratory door against the intrusion of unsuspecting visitors. He wrapped the cathode ray tube in heavy, black-painted cardboard so that the light originating from within the tube itself would not hinder his observations. Once all was prepared, Roentgen shut off the lights and allowed his eyes to accommodate to the darkness.

When Roentgen powered up the tube that evening, he was surprised to see a faint glimmer of light coming from an object leaning against a nearby wall. He confirmed the source of the glow: a piece of cardboard on which he had painted barium platinocyanide, a substance known to fluoresce when exposed to cathode rays. Given the popularity at the time of experimenting with vacuum tubes, it is highly likely that others, including Lenard, observed a similar effect during their investigations; but if they did, they must have either ignored it or erroneously attributed what they had seen to cathode rays. They committed the cardinal sin of science: they paid more attention to what they expected to see than what they actually saw. It was Roentgen who recognized the significance of his observation. The glowing plate was several feet away from the cathode ray tube. This was farther than cathode rays were known to travel. Dismissing cathode rays as the agent causing the fluorescence, Roentgen correctly deduced that he was witnessing a previously unreported phenomenon. What Roentgen experienced was the convergence of serendipity and a mind open to new possibilities, arriving at what we might today call an "aha moment."

Roentgen must have considered immediately reporting his observations. However, if he had, he would have risked Lenard and other scientists making the connection and carrying out the critical experiments that would secure Roentgen's place in scientific history. Instead, in Roentgen's own words, "I didn't think, I investigated." He did so alone, staving off the very human urge to tell someone —anyone—about what he quickly recognized was a discovery of far-reaching importance. "I had spoken to no one about my work," he later wrote. "To my wife [Anna Bertha, whom he called "Bertha"], I merely mentioned that I was working on something about which people would say when they found out about it, 'Roentgen has surely gone crazy.'"

Soon, though, Bertha knew something was up. Several nights after his initial observation, Roentgen asked her to come to his laboratory, perhaps the first time he had ever made such an unusual request. From that first night of discovery, he'd begun to study the properties of the new rays. Perhaps his most amazing observation, which he now wished to further investigate, was that when he waved his hand between the tube and the barium platinocyanide–coated placard, he could see a ghostly image of what appeared to be the bones of his fingers and wrist.

When Bertha arrived, her husband seated her beside a table. Without explanation, he affixed his wife's hand to a photographic plate. He then exposed her to what we now know to be an unconscionable fifteen minutes of unshielded irradiation. The resultant image—the first human radiograph—has become iconic. Clearly visible are the bones of Bertha's hand, her wedding band encircling her marital finger. When her husband showed her the photograph, she is said to have uttered the words, "I have seen my death."

Working alone and in continuing secrecy, Roentgen elicited much of what we know today about X-rays. His initial, December 28, 1895, publication, "On a New Kind of Rays," was a remarkable reflection of the man himself, modest and reserved to the point of reticence. Without verbal embroidery, Roentgen let his readers decide for themselves the worth of his discovery. Some of the principle properties the publication detailed were that X-rays:

- Are invisible to the naked eye;
- Neither reflect nor refract in the manner of visible light;
- Are unresponsive to magnetic fields;
- Are absorbed in direct relationship to the density and thickness of the objects they encounter.

Roentgen's report on the new rays was soon republished in English in *Nature*, *Science*, and *Scientific American*, but by then the word was out. On New Year's Day 1896, Roentgen mailed ninety copies of his article to well-known scientists and colleagues throughout Europe. In twelve of the missives, sent to those whom he felt would be the most supportive, he included a packet of nine photographs. Among them was the image of Bertha's hand.

One of the recipients, Franz-Serafin Exner, had been a university classmate of Roentgen in Zurich and was now a professor of experimental physics in Vienna. Exner showed the photographs to a friend whose father was Ernst Lecher, the publisher of *Die Presse*, Vienna's leading daily newspaper. Lecher knew a good story when he saw one. Realizing that he had a scoop, he literally stopped the presses, made room on the front page, and published the story of Roentgen's findings the very next day under the headline "A Sensational Discovery." With remarkable prescience, Lecher predicted, "If we let our imaginations run freely . . . this could be of immeasurable help for the diagnosis of countless diseases."

Viennese correspondents for other newspapers trumpeted the news to their home publications around the world. The press expanded upon

Lecher's prediction. London's *Daily Chronicle* waxed, "A sensational discovery, which, if the reports are confirmed, is likely to be attended by imperial consequences for physical and medical science." *The Standard* assured its readers, "There is no hoax or humbug in this matter." Despite Roentgen's preference for the term "X-rays," to imply their mysterious nature, the press dubbed the emanations "Roentgen rays." As later happened with Eddington's verification of Einstein's prediction about the bending of light, the public embraced both the discovery and the discoverer, seemingly overnight.

The initial response of the scientific community was tepid. However, skepticism vanished quickly following the events of January 23, 1896. That evening, the Physical and Medical Society of Wuerzburg held a symposium on the new rays in the main lecture hall of the University of Wuerzburg's Institute for Physics. At the conclusion of a comprehensive presentation of his observations, Roentgen called forward a well-known anatomist named Geheimrat Albert von Kolliker. As he had with his wife Bertha, Roentgen imaged the scientist's hand. Imagine the amazement of those attending the evening's events. They had not simply heard about the new rays but witnessed a most dramatic exhibition of their potential. On the platinocyanide plate, the image of von Kolliker's hand is crisp and sharp. It appears broad and squat in comparison with Bertha's. His fourth digit bears not one ring, as with Bertha's hand, but two. Von Kolliker called for three cheers from the crowd and, to unanimous acclaim, immediately suggested that the new rays be named for their discoverer.

There followed an outpouring of professional admiration. The University of Wuerzburg conferred on Roentgen its most exalted honor, naming him rector of the university. The students held a celebratory torchlight parade, insisting the notoriously shy professor regale them with a speech. He received various national medals and opportunities to lecture around the world. In 1901, Roentgen was awarded the first Nobel Prize for physics. His discovery spawned the entirely new field of medical imaging, or diagnostic radiology, with all of its subsequent developments—ultrasonography, computed tomography, magnetic resonance imaging, and nuclear medicine—traceable to that single instant of recognition in 1895.

Within months of Roentgen's discovery, X-rays found their principal application in medicine. In Glasgow, Dr. John McIntyre showed the potential of medical imaging to demonstrate the presence of kidney stones and swallowed foreign objects. His work was emulated at the Dartmouth Infirmary in the United States by Dr. Edwin Frost, who showed the advantages of roentgenographic imaging in diagnosing broken bones. The Roentgen rays found extensive medical applications during the Boer War and in World War I. Marie Curie famously spent the money she received with her second Nobel Prize on a mobile X-ray machine that she drove along the front lines, exposing radiographs to improve the treatment of wounded soldiers.

X-ray frenzy extended beyond medical applications. Before it was recognized that overlong and repetitive exposure to X-radiation was acutely injurious and, with excessive exposure, might induce cancer in the long term, entrepreneurs seeking to capitalize on Roentgen's discovery employed X-rays in new consumer products and even entertainment. Pitchmen ballyhooed harmless but ineffectual home remedies containing fluids they said had been exposed to X-rays as curative for everyday ills like headaches and constipation. Fears developed that the dissemination of X-ray apparatuses would infringe on personal privacy. There were rumors that X-rays would allow the unscrupulous to see through women's clothing, prompting one company to quite profitably sell a line of X-ray-proof garments. A bit of doggerel played upon this conceit:

> For now-a-days I hear they'll gaze,
> Through cloak and gown and even stays,
> Those naughty, naughty Roentgen Rays.

As Roentgen's popularity grew, Lenard stewed from the sidelines. Lenard eventually received his Nobel Prize in 1905 for the work he'd done with high-energy vacuum tubes, but that did not reverse the public perception. The press glorified Roentgen, while the name "Lenard" hardly bore mention. He had missed the big discovery and received short shrift. Despite his having done the work that had made possible the discovery of the X-ray, next to Roentgen, he was comparatively an unknown.

Lenard's experience with Roentgen presaged his attacks on Einstein by a quarter of a century. How unfair! It had been his contributions that underlay everything that Roentgen had described. Roentgen had been lucky; his discovery was simply the logical next step to the groundwork Lenard had laid. Lenard didn't fault a giddy and naïve public. It wasn't their fault that they were ignorant of the complete story. It was Roentgen. Why hadn't Roentgen set the record straight by giving him credit as a full partner, for being the one who had enabled his observations?

Lenard's relationship with Roentgen, as with Einstein, began benignly, even with admiration. In an early letter written by Roentgen to Lenard in 1894, Roentgen expressed a desire to acquire some of the aluminum windows that Lenard was using on his eponymous tube. Lenard answered apologetically that the machinist he was using was having trouble enough supplying his own needs, but nonetheless, "I permit myself to send you two sheets from my supply."

Three years after Roentgen announced his discovery, Lenard wrote him a letter, declaring, "I was particularly happy to know for sure what I had never had reason to doubt, that you are friendly toward me. I was often afraid it could have been otherwise, and I would have been sorry for that." Absolving himself from any "polemics" that may have come to Roentgen's attention, Lenard continued, "Because your remarkable discovery caused such remarkable attention in the farthest circles, my modest work also has come into the limelight, which was of particular luck to me, and I am doubly glad to have had your friendly participation, *especially through the presence of the x-ray discovered by you* [italics mine]." He acknowledged that he had erred by presuming the observed effects were due to cathode rays rather than X-rays. By giving Roentgen credit for the initial discovery, Lenard provided history with a literal smoking gun that went against Lenard's later assertions that he was the discoverer of X-rays.

For his part, Roentgen portrayed a similar tone of collegiality and respect. A letter to Lenard written in April 1897 expressed disappointment at his not being in Wuerzburg to receive Lenard when the younger man unexpectedly came to visit. "I hope there will soon be another opportunity," Roentgen wrote. "For the receipt of prizes and medals we several times have had reason for mutual congratulations. . . . Be assured that I am very happy that my work has found such a ready recognition from you."

Roentgen further apologized for "untimely newspaper articles" written by a former assistant and close friend, Ludwig Zehnder, whom he had known since his days as a student. He had complained in a letter to Zehnder about rumors to the effect that it was not he, Roentgen, who had discovered the X-ray but an assistant or *diener*. He now wrote Lenard that he had mentioned Lenard's name only in passing and that he was "innocent as a newborn child and furious about it."

Curiously, while Roentgen's will ordered the destruction of his papers after his death in 1923, he insisted that his correspondence with Lenard be preserved in a safe at the University of Wuerzburg, presumably over concerns about the younger man's claims to the historical provenance of X-rays. It was well that he did. During the 1930s, the years of Lenard's greatest influence with the Nazi hierarchy, fears arose among Roentgen's Wuerzburg colleagues that pro-Lenard elements might seek to destroy the letters. Authorities at the Institute made photocopies and sent them to sympathetic scientists in other locales for safekeeping.

Their caution was well founded. As Lenard's political star ascended, he became more assertive in his claims of primacy regarding the discovery of X-rays. The scientific establishment of the Third Reich sought to revise the history surrounding the events of 1895. In 1935, an article by Johannes Stark concluded that Roentgen had done little that was original. Rather, he had merely followed in the footsteps of Lenard. Assistant professor Friedrich Schmidt, working under Stark, who by then had become president of Berlin's powerful Reich Physical and Technical Institute, also sided with Lenard. He concluded that despite a lack of physical evidence, Lenard had made notes indicative of his having recognized X-rays for what they were prior to Roentgen's first publication.

Roentgen believed that his receiving the Nobel Prize for discovering X-rays precipitated Lenard's envy, but there may have been multiple factors at work. Given his suspicious nature, Lenard may well have held a grudge over Roentgen's letter to Zehnder, believing that, despite his disclaimer, Roentgen had written negative comments about him that later found their way into the public sphere. Even more critically, as was evident with his envy of Einstein's accolades, he almost certainly made resentful comparisons between Roentgen's public acclaim and his own. Even his own Nobel Prize failed to salve the hurt he felt over the recognition accorded Roentgen. He belittled Roentgen's contributions in his Nobel Lecture and took the position that "anyone who was wide awake and using a Lenard tube could have discovered the X-rays."

If Lenard's claims of primacy depend on Roentgen having used a Lenard tube that evening in 1895 when he intuited X-rays, then they lack supporting evidence. The type of tube Roentgen was using when he made the leap from observation to discovery is unknown. An investigation of purchasing records shows that the University of Wuerzburg Institute of Physics bought only one Lenard tube in 1895, but at the same time acquired a number of Hittorf and Crookes tubes. The type of tube Roentgen employed the night of November 8, 1895, remains a point of contention.

Given Lenard's statements concerning the inevitability of Roentgen's discovery, why didn't he discover X-rays? According to Lenard's laboratory workbooks, it appears he had, on occasion, observed what he believed to be cathode rays causing imprints on photographic plates. He also had witnessed plates fluorescing at distances greater than would be expected of cathode rays and after traversing objects that would have been expected to stop their less energetic passage.

Lenard gave four reasons why he missed out on being the discoverer of X-rays, three of which were parroted by Stark in a 1935 publication when Stark and Lenard were at the peak of their influence. That the items are worded nearly identically suggests that Lenard colluded with Stark in making his own case:

1. During that period when he was serving a sequence of temporary appointments, he had changed institutions so frequently that he had not had the time to settle in and conduct his experiments as he would have liked;

2. At the time, he was using a tube encased in tin to exclude light emissions, rather than the cardboard used by Roentgen; the tin might have absorbed more of the X-rays, thus reducing their intensity;

3. He was at the mercy of Professor Hertz. The professor preferred he use a cheaper substance—keton (pentadecylparatolylketon), rather than barium platinocyanide—for his investigations. In fact, experiments conducted by Roentgen validated the seriousness of this shortcoming. Roentgen found that although keton fluoresced remarkably well under the bombardment of cathode rays, the material was wholly unresponsive to X-rays;

4. His cathode ray tube was poorly made by the glassblower, Louis Mueller-Unkel, whereas Roentgen's tube had been made perfectly. In this regard, Lenard again blamed Hertz for his stinginess. Lenard wrote in his autobiography that he had approached his professor about purchasing a better tube. While Hertz had not said "no" outright, he clearly was unconvinced, telling the young man to go forward with the purchase only if he felt that the new tube would truly be worth the expense.

These last two explanations require further scrutiny. The half-Jew Hertz had prevented him from having been the first to observe X-rays and reap the recognition that had been accorded Roentgen. On the other hand, despite Hertz's racial heritage, his story, at least, is included among Lenard's summaries in his book about the lives and scientific works of "great men." The biographies of neither Roentgen nor Einstein are among the sixty-one selected.

As Hitler's chief scientific advisor, Lenard remained a powerful force in German academic politics and among the scientists of the Third Reich long after his 1933 retirement from his directorship of the University of Heidelberg Institute of Physics. To insinuate doubt about the authenticity of Roentgen's claims, he repeatedly raised the question: why had Roentgen insisted on his executors burning his research notebooks and other papers upon his death? Subsequent articles in Nazi periodicals like *Voelkischer Beobachter* and *Das Schwarze Korps*—the weekly publication of the SS—beat the drum for official recognition of Lenard as the discoverer of X-rays until the Reich happily complied.

The Nazis did their best to eradicate the memory of Roentgen's work and replace it with an ersatz history that lauded one of their own. In 1944, the same Physical and Medical Society of Wuerzburg, before whom Roentgen first presented his discovery, made application to the Minister of the Reichspost (the German postal service), Wilhelm Ohnesorge, requesting that the Reich design a stamp honoring the fiftieth anniversary of Roentgen's discovery. Ohnesorge was coincidentally a physicist who had trained under Lenard. The request was denied.

In 1945, as American troops advanced toward Berlin during the final days of World War II, Lenard fled Heidelberg. Along with Stark, he had been one of the point men involved in enforcing laws forbidding the employment of Jews in German universities. He was certain that those charged with seeking out and detaining Nazi war criminals would be on the lookout for him. Surprisingly to Lenard, they either were not looking for him or were oblivious of his whereabouts. He remained at large for nearly two months in the tiny Badensian farming village of Messelhausen before turning himself in to authorities and being placed under house arrest.

A little more than a month later, Lieutenant Colonel Lewis E. Etter, an American physician of the U.S. Army Medical Reserve Corps, sat in the anteroom of Lenard's cottage. Doctor Etter had requested and been given permission through military channels to conduct two interviews of Philipp Lenard about his relationship with Wilhelm Conrad Roentgen, the man credited everywhere except Nazi Germany with discovering X-rays. Lenard's claims to the contrary had come up during a trip to Roentgen's laboratory in Wuerzburg, earlier in the year. Etter's interest in Lenard was academic. While stationed in England, early in the war, he had made an extensive study of radiation physics. Later, he served as chief of radiology at several military medical installations in Europe. He was only months away from resuming his civilian life as a neuroradiology fellow and an instructor in radiology at the University of Pittsburgh. In time,

Etter would become a leading expert on the radiographic anatomy of the skull.

On September 20, 1945, Etter sat enveloped in an overstuffed chair beside a dark wood table, lamplight reflecting from its oiled sheen. Only a moment earlier, he had closed the thick volume lying beside him. From his first interview of Lenard two weeks earlier and after reading parts of Lenard's *Deutsche Physik*, which the aged scientist had suggested he borrow from a local physician, Etter had learned the essence of the old man's dispute with Roentgen. He'd found a handwritten note, signed by Lenard, on the flyleaf of the book:

> To be found in this volume, my reckoning with Roentgen, held back for almost fifty years. . . . Again, I speak now only because of my ineradicable desire for truth. For fifty long years one was so dull as never to care seriously about the actual coming about of a rather much noticed and practically used discovery.

Having familiarized himself with the history that lay between the two men, Etter felt that he had prepared himself as much as possible. He'd read the passages he'd found cited in Lenard's note and felt that he now understood Lenard's point of view. He'd also read and reread a footnote he'd found well into the text: "A comparison can best make clear to the neutral observer Roentgen's role in the discovery," Lenard wrote. He went on,

> I shall make this striking comparison here because it may throw a light on the even now widespread historical confusion and untruth! Roentgen was the midwife at the birth of the discovery. This helper had the good fortune to be able to present the child first. She can only be confused with the mother by the uninformed who knows as little about the procedure of the discovery and the preceding facts as children of the stork.

Etter reopened Lenard's book and took another glance at the flyleaf. From his first interview of Lenard, it was clear that Lenard's position on the discovery of X-rays was unchanged. On that occasion, he had expressed the same birthing metaphor as he had written but even more directly. He was the true "mother of the X-rays." Lenard's work had guided Roentgen to the point that "All Roentgen had to do was push a button, since all the groundwork had been prepared by me. . . . Without my help, the discovery of X-rays would not have been possible even today. Without me, the name of Roentgen would be unknown."

The second interview continued for some time in the same vein. Lenard was in high spirits at the interest the American soldier showed in his life. They were covering well-trod ground when Lenard made an additional claim. Speaking of the history of cathode ray tubes, he credited Hittorf with the initial invention, then added, "But nothing of great importance was added to it until my work twenty-five years later. I was always too modest and did not rush into print. In my letter to Roentgen, where I praised him for his great discovery [the letter of May 21, 1897], I thought he would reply that he really owed it all to me and my tube, but I waited for this acknowledgement from him in vain."

Etter was stunned. He recognized in that instant that this was the main source of Lenard's resentment for Roentgen—not that Roentgen had scooped him on the discovery but that he felt slighted by not having been invited to share the glory. Was this all of what had motivated Lenard's long crusade to minimize Roentgen's achievement? Or was there something even more nefarious? Etter was well aware that Lenard had had a hand in war crimes against Jewish academics. He had read something of Lenard's rambling polemic detailing his beliefs concerning the degeneracy of the Jewish race in his introduction to *Deutsche Physik*. Etter wondered if there might also be an element of anti-Semitism involved in his perception of Roentgen. He asked the question directly, "Was Roentgen a Jew?"

Lenard replied, "No, but he was a friend of Jews and acted like one."

There was little more to say. As Etter stood to leave, Lenard asked that the Lieutenant Colonel wait just a moment and left the room. He returned a couple of minutes later and formally presented Etter with a photographic portrait of himself taken three years previously on his eightieth birthday. It had been a marvelous day for Lenard, immensely brightened by a personal congratulatory communication from Adolf Hitler. The portrait depicted Lenard in formal attire, his chin lifted proudly, his eyes gazing skyward. On the back of the photograph, Lenard had inscribed, "Dr. Etter, the representative of the conqueror, with thanks for his scientific interest. 20 Sept. 45," and signed it "P. Lenard."

7

LENARD IN STOCKHOLM

"Your Majesty, Your Royal Highness, Ladies and Gentlemen," announced Professor A. Lindstedt. "The Royal Swedish Academy of Sciences has decided to give this year's Nobel Prize for physics to Dr. Philipp Lenard, Professor at the University of Kiel, for his important work on cathode rays." Lenard stood beside Lindstedt. At the mention of his name, he bent slightly at the waist and favored the audience with a thin, tight-lipped smile.

The presentation of the Nobel Prizes on this dark, cold evening of December 10, 1905, had filled every seat of the main concert hall of Stockholm's Academy of Music. Sweden's King Oscar II and his Queen, Sophia of Nassau, sat behind Lindstedt and Lenard on the stage, seemingly intent on the distinguished scientist's every pronouncement. King Oscar was a patron of science and culture, and was himself an amateur writer and musician. He had taken a very personal interest in the Nobel ceremonies since they'd begun five years earlier, when Alfred Nobel's heirs had finally exhausted the available legal obstructions to exercising the dictates of the great man's will.

Having invented dynamite and holding three hundred fifty-five other patents at the time of his death in 1896, Nobel had been a very wealthy man. His last will, signed the previous year at the Swedish-Norwegian Club in Paris, left the majority of his fortune—roughly 31.6 million Swedish kronor (equivalent to about USD $255 million in 2013)—for the establishment of a fund. The interest from the fund was to be used to award significant monetary prizes that Nobel hoped would both incentivize important work and recognize the achievements of men and women that "shall have conferred the greatest benefit on mankind." More specifically, Nobel's will stipulated that the interest accrued from his bequest, each year, be divided among persons "who shall have made the most important discovery or invention" within the fields of physics, chemistry, and medicine or physiology; "who shall have produced in the field of literature the most outstanding work in an ideal direction"; and who had most contributed to activities intended to promote peace among nations.

Lindstedt continued with his introduction of Lenard,

> The discovery of the cathode rays forms the first link in the chain of brilliant discoveries with which the names of Roentgen, Becquerel, and Curie are connected. The discovery itself was made by Hittorf as long ago as 1869 and therefore falls in a period before that which the Nobel Foundation is able to take into account. However, the recognition which Lenard has earned himself by the further development of Hittorf's discovery (which is becoming of increasing importance) shows that he too deserves the same reward as has already come to several of his successors for work of a similar nature.

Lindstedt laid out the background of experimentation that preceded and influenced Lenard's work, then ticked off the principal contributions that had brought Lenard to the exalted state of Nobel Prize honoree. Perhaps foremost, Lenard had, in a sense, reinvented the cathode ray tube and made its use more efficient by replacing the glass at the cathode end of the tube with a thin aluminum plate. The plate allowed the rays to pass through so that "it became possible to study cathode rays under much simpler and more convenient experimental conditions than before." He found no differences in the rays within the tube versus those that had passed through the aluminum window. Moreover, the cathode rays "proved to be carriers of negative electricity even in empty space, and they could be deflected from their path by both magnetic and electrical fields." Finally, Lenard found differences among the cathode rays based on the extent to which they were generated in a vacuum and could be deflected by a magnet.

In wrapping up, Lindstedt projected the future importance of Lenard's discoveries. His research raised questions about how cathode rays were propagated. Were they supported by an ether, as Lenard proposed? Or perhaps, as the Englishman Crookes had suggested, the rays were comprised of electrons moving at very high speeds. "It is clear," Lindstedt concluded, "that Lenard's work on cathode rays has not only enriched our knowledge of these phenomena, but has also served in many respects as a basis for the development of the electron theory. Lenard's discovery that cathode rays can exist outside the discharge tube, in particular, has opened up new fields of research in physics."

As Lindstedt completed his remarks, he turned to Lenard, shook his hand, and spoke a few personal congratulatory words. The Swede crossed the stage to hand King Oscar the ornate certificate and gold medal symbolizing the award, and the King, in turn, presented them to Lenard. Lenard smiled broadly to receive the applause of the crowd.

As he returned to his seat, he thought he should feel more exhilarated, but it was all over so quickly, his moment in the sun. The papers would carry the story of the ceremony in the morning, but nothing would really change for him. A few days hence, the general public will already have forgotten the name Lenard. Still, how many men in their lifetime received such an honor? And there was the prize money to consider—one hundred-thirty eight thousand Swedish kronor—which, with the expense of having a family, was sorely needed. He forced a smile, but it didn't feel quite right. In all fairness, he really should have received the very first Nobel Prize, the one Roentgen had stolen from him in 1901. At the very least, he had deserved to share it with Roentgen.

Lenard had heard what he knew to be more than a rumor. The committee responsible for vetting the nominations for the physics prize had recommended that he and Roentgen share the 1901 award, but the committee had been voted down by the main assembly on a technicality. A faction of the assembly had argued that, at least for the first prize, there should be only a single honoree. Roentgen might have stepped forward and voiced his support for Lenard; he'd had every opportunity to give the proper credit. Instead, Roentgen had been greedy and showed his true colors. He had been so wrapped up in the public acclaim for his discovery that he'd forgotten it was purely an accident. No one would ever have heard of Roentgen except that Lenard's work had led him by his nose to the obvious. Apparently, rightfully sharing the responsibility for the discovery of X-rays never occurred to him. Worse. Perhaps it did.

He felt a small thrill of pride over the Nobel Prizes awarded to his countrymen who followed him onto the stage—Adolf von Baeyer for his work in organic chemistry and Robert Koch, who received the Nobel Prize in Medicine or Physiology for his research into the pathogenesis of tuberculosis. Germans had swept the prizes in the sciences, the only ones that mattered.

A Pole had won the Prize for literature. Lenard looked again at his program to remind himself of the man's name. Henryk Sienkiewicz. The presenter, this time a man introduced as the Permanent Secretary of the Swedish Academy, had prattled on inanely about what really was nothing more than inconsequential scribbling. The way the presenter was gushing over the new laureate was embarrassing: "in every nation there are some rare geniuses who concentrate in themselves the spirit of the nation." Rubbish! And then, "Their inspiration is deeply rooted in the past, like the oak tree of Baublis in the desert of Lithuania." What effete babble! He had known since childhood that mathematics and the natural sciences were all that really mattered. He had written that these subjects were the "oases within the desert. . . . All the getting up at four in the morning and going to bed at midnight was of no use—history and geography did not enter my head."

There had been more speeches that night, but Lenard hardly paid them any attention. It was amazing, the unexpected twists that had brought him to such grand heights. His father had wanted him to take over the family wine business. Lenard had hated the very idea of it. There had been quite a few arguments over his resistance. To appease the old man, he'd given it a try after his initial scientific training. He'd read some biographies of famous scientists whose investigations were sidelights to other careers.

Perhaps he could emulate them. In the end, he couldn't do it. Working in a business had been beneath him, so bourgeois, so Jewish. Jews were said to be good at business. He wasn't so sure. His father's partner had been a Jew, a man named Leban, but still the business had failed.

Science had been his first and only love. As a boy, he had routinely saved some of the small allowance his parents gave him. When he had saved enough, he wandered down to the Krapp brothers' bookshop at the edge of Pressburg's Jewish quarter and spent his money on whatever science book caught his attention. It was an awful shame when the store went under. He'd gone to Steiner's after that. By then, his interest in science was in full flight. He had built a chemistry laboratory in his parents' garden and conducted experiments. Years later, when he was in high school, his teacher, Virgil Klatt, had taken him under his wing. During school and even on holidays, they had performed hundreds of experiments together, reproducing Becquerel's work with phosphorescent stones.

He'd tried to take his doctoral degree at the University of Budapest but wasn't admitted. Bunsen accepted him at Heidelberg, where he received his degree with high honors in 1886. By then, he'd already established a reputation as a man who bore watching. Still, it hadn't been easy finding a permanent position until Kiel had taken a chance on him. He'd spent a year or two in each of a number of temporary positions—Berlin with Helmholtz, then Budapest, Aachen, and Breslau, before his temporary appointment at Heidelberg in 1896. By this point in his career, he'd already been credited with what was called the "waterfall effect" by some and the "Lenard effect" by others. He had to admit that the latter had a nice ring to it. His experiments had revealed the separation of positive and negative electrical charges as water droplets broke up while falling through the atmosphere, and described the differing shapes of water droplets depending on their size.

He'd begun his work with cathode ray tubes when he was with Helmholtz, in Berlin, during 1888. His invention of the "Lenard window," while he was still in his twenties, had made his career. The window was simply an opening in the cathode end of the glass tube covered by a thin aluminum foil that allowed better egress of the cathode rays outside the tube for improved study. It was only a short step from this point to his discovery of the photoelectric effect. He'd found that the interaction of ultraviolet light and a metal plate caused the release of energy according to the frequency of the light. The result surprised him, as he had expected there to be a much stronger correlation with the intensity of the light; the exact nature of the relationship remained obscure. Had he heard that there was a young man in Zurich who had worked on this exact problem? It seemed to him that he had.

His path to success had been a long road with many false turns and disappointments, but he had persevered. The universities that had not kept him on the faculty, that had encouraged him to try elsewhere, had made a grave mistake. The Nobel Prize was proof of that.

Lenard was roused from his thoughts by people standing and moving around him. The presentation ceremony was over. Lindstedt was hovering, greeting the sycophants wishing to have a word with him as though he had been the one awarded the prize. He saw in the distance the royals, Oscar and Sophia, leaving with their retinue for the banquet. The crowd trailed, looking wolfish, as though they had not eaten in days.

Lenard followed the crowd outside to the dining room of a nearby hotel and found his assigned place among the hundreds of dinner guests. Despite his mood, he couldn't help but marvel at the surrounding finery. The women wore long gowns of every imaginable color and design, many purchased at the best Parisian shops. Adding to their elegance, they had donned their finest wool and fur stoles, white gloves that ascended their arms to their elbows and beyond, and glittering gems retrieved earlier that day from household vaults and secret hiding places scattered among the best neighborhoods in Stockholm.

In contrast, the men were nearly uniformly attired, each wearing, as he was, a long-tailed, black cutaway jacket paired with matching slacks featuring black cords up the outside of the legs, a stiff white shirt with a white wing collar, and either white or silver cuff links and shirt studs. The more rakish sported a white pocket square conservatively extruding just the slightest amount from their left breast pocket.

Lenard seated himself and greeted the guests beside and across from him. The ballroom was dazzling. Long rectangular tables were lined up end to end in long, straight rows and covered with expensive linens. Arrangements of exotic flowers, imported from warmer climes, soared upward at regular intervals. Each guest's place had been set with fine china, an array of silverware, organized from the periphery inward to receive each course in order, and a selection of leaded Orrefors crystal, gleaming in candlelight. Less than a decade old, the company had designed special glassware to commemorate the event. Each style was specifically shaped to maximize the enjoyment of the wine that would accompany each serving.

Suddenly, from the kitchen, came a burst of activity. Gaggles of waiters, dressed in dinner jackets and carrying decorative bowls of beef consommé, circled behind the diners to reach over their left shoulders and deposit their burdens. The same choreography brought forth, at intervals, a sequence of filet of sole, saddle of lamb, hot and cold partridge, and hearts of artichoke, followed by ice cream, pastry and fruit. Each course was paired with a carefully selected wine—Golden Sherry, Chateau Doutor, a Hochheimer white wine, champagne by Mumm, Romanee from Burgundy, Apollonaris with dessert, and Sandeman port with cigars. The remarkable display of excess emphasized the day's theme: these were extraordinary men who had earned this evening's special culinary tribute.

Lord knows, he had done the work—and then he had waited. Only a very select group of scientists had the right to make Nobel nominations: members of the Nobel physics committee or of the Royal Swedish Academy of Sciences; past Nobel laureates; professors of physics in Scandinavian countries; and holders of chairs in a selected cadre of Scandinavian institutions. Lenard's name had been bruited around the assembly as a candidate from the start. In 1901, all five members of the physics committee had suggested both his name and Roentgen's. He had received additional support from the British physicist and mathematician Sylvanus Thompson, a foreign member of the Swedish Academy, but it had not been enough to carry the day. For the next four years, a man who would become his collaborator in his quest to prove the existence of ether,

Vilhelm Bjerknes, nominated him for the prize. In 1904, two other scientists—Wiener and Hallwachs—had placed his name in nomination, although they both proffered additional nominations at the same time.

This year, it had been Bjerknes again, but also Jacobus van't Hoff, the Dutch professor who had won the very first prize for chemistry. It must have been van't Hoff who had done the trick. It galled Lenard that it had taken so long for the Nobel committee to recognize him. Professor Lindstedt had unwittingly made the case in his introduction, saying Lenard was responsible for providing the foundation from which Roentgen's and the Curies' research had sprung. His work had come first; he had led the way. Then he had looked on from the sidelines as each of those who had followed and benefited from his discoveries had been selected before him. Yet, despite Lenard's work lying at the root of so much of modern physics, there had been no mass acclaim for him as there had been for Roentgen, and for Becquerel and the Curies too, for that matter.

What initially had been an almost inconsequential slight had inadvertently been imprinted on his consciousness by Professor Lindstedt. Now, he could not let it go. That the others had prospered by feeding off his ideas rankled to such an extent that by May 28 of the following year, when Lenard returned to Stockholm to deliver the traditional Nobel Lecture, "On Cathode Rays," he was ready to set the record straight. He had stood by and watched Roentgen take the credit for what was rightfully his for long enough.

"I shall now speak not only of the fruits but also of the trees which have borne them, and of those who planted these trees," Lenard began. "This approach is the more suitable in my case, as I have by no means always been numbered among those who pluck the fruit; I have been repeatedly only one of those who planted or cared for the trees, or who helped to do this."

The lecture progressed historically through his research, addressing how cathode rays varied according to different combinations of metals and tube designs until he reached this particularly salient passage: "It is barely worth mentioning, but not unimportant for the further development of our subject, that even before this interruption [the death of his mentor,

Heinrich Hertz], I had designed a new and far more convenient type of discharge tube. I had tested it as far as possible and had recommended its use and made it generally available."

Lenard's tube employed platinum as the cathode target, which he claimed was the material that produced the greatest number of X-rays. Between the efficiency of the platinum plate and his tube design, which allowed the X-rays generated by the high-energy electrons striking the plate to freely exit the tube, he dismissively concluded, "The discovery soon after this of X-rays by Roentgen, the first investigator to use the type of tube described above, is generally considered to be a good example of a lucky discovery. But, given the tube, the fact that the attention of the observer was already turned from the interior to the outside of the tube, and the presence of phosphorescent screens outside the tube, because of the purpose of the tube, it appeared to me that this discovery had of necessity to be made at this stage of development." In plain language, Lenard was claiming that it was his work had led Roentgen to his discovery. Any fool could have done it. It just so happened that Roentgen was the fool who did.

This indictment of Roentgen as merely "lucky" and beholden to Lenard for his good fortune was a typical one for Lenard. In time, Lenard would come to have similar complaints about Einstein and his law of the photoelectric effect. Ironically, in 1905, the same year that Lenard sat on the Nobel stage, the scientific world would read Albert Einstein's article in *Annalen der Physik* on the law of the photoelectric effect. It had been Lenard who had first written about the curious effect several years earlier, but he had not been able to elucidate the physical laws that governed it. Using the constant derived by Max Planck, it was left to Einstein to bring forth the relationship between the wavelength, or frequency, of ultraviolet light striking a metal plate and the kinetic energy of the electrons released as a result.

Given that he was widely celebrated as one of the great scientists of his era, it seems surprising that Philipp Lenard so begrudged the recognition accorded the contributions of his contemporaries. However, this was his character. Toward the end of his career, Lenard kept a *Faelschungs-*

Buch, a cataloging of what he believed were the ideas stolen from him by his colleagues. A handwritten note found within the covers of the book states,

> They who could have understood my works most easily have obviously never appreciated [what I have done]. This was astonishing to me; however, I understood it soon enough by their and their students' statements in their publications. They aggressively tried as much to conceal me as to tacitly rob me! How do they come to behave like that? . . . They probably have all been that way, these "colleagues." Thus they could not be delighted by my works, their methods and results; but they were anxious for their pleasant positions, and so a counter fight seemed to be the best for them in the first place! So they behaved in any case.

Despite the stilted, archaic style of writing, Lenard's disappointment, even anger, over the behavior of his fellow academics is palpable. He appears to have given up on them. He is writing for posterity.

> The here preserved publications show it. I have preserved them and continue to do so, because they are tangible proof of a behavior (which one probably has to have at hand) which seemed so alien to me that I even sometimes had to (being forgetful) consider as incredible. . . . There are some publications, which only followed the recent widely employed trend to bypass me. One, even a pupil of mine, deceived me from behind, because he deemed it beneficial for himself. . . . That they have been able to behave in the way they did, these poor minds owe to the Jewish influence, which became effective just in time and by which their petty-minded thinking became as strong, as they could ever wish for.

On the occasion of his Nobel Lecture, he felt it necessary to give voice to his resentment over the acclaim Roentgen enjoyed for his discovery. One can only imagine the embarrassed response of his audience: Philipp Lenard, the great scientist, a Nobel laureate, denigrating the contributions of another Nobel Prize recipient in an effort to bolster his own legacy.

Lenard's behavior toward Roentgen and, later, Einstein would follow him through history. Indeed, instead of being remembered for the genius of his science, his legacy is his misbegotten racial theories and how they negatively impacted the future of German science. His modern-day Nobel biography notes, "Some of his discoveries were great ones and others were very important, but he claimed for them more than their true value. Although he was given many honours . . . he believed that he was disregarded and this probably explains why he attacked other physicists in many countries."

8

EINSTEIN VERSUS THE
SMALL POPES IN UPPSALA

Seventeen years following Lenard's Nobel Lecture, on the afternoon of July 11, 1923, Albert Einstein looked out from the elevated podium fronting Jubileum Hall, prepared to deliver his own Nobel Lecture. The newly finished building was an architectural marvel, completely walled in glass, and one of the focal points of Gothenburg's Liseberg Congress Center, which, along with the neighboring amusement park, had been constructed to celebrate the city's three hundredth anniversary. For the next hour, those fortunate or persistent enough to have gotten a ticket forsook the park's funicular and slides to listen to the 1921 Nobel laureate for physics.

The day was an unusually hot one for central Sweden, hot enough that Einstein's neck must have prickled under his stiff, white collar. The freshly lacquered benches on which the audience sat stuck to the trousers of their expensive wool suits. Even so, roughly one thousand scientists, dignitaries, and guests sat mesmerized through the roughly hour-long presentation. Among them was Sweden's King Gustav V, who occupied a special chair in the central aisle separating the left and right sections.

Beyond the unseasonable warmth, there were several interesting oddities about the circumstances of Einstein's celebratory lecture. First, Einstein had known about his being awarded the Nobel Prize for nearly a year, but only now was he getting around to delivering his lecture. Second, the award Einstein received was the 1921 Nobel Prize for physics, a year already fogged by distant memory. Stalemated discussions among the Nobel physics committee members over who should be the recipient of the 1921 physics award resulted in the prize being held in reserve until a decision was made during the committee's usual deliberations held in 1922. Third, Einstein's host in Gothenburg, Svante Arrhenius, had on several occasions in his capacity as a member of the Nobel physics committee assessed Einstein's dossier as unworthy of a Nobel Prize. Arrhenius had arranged for Einstein's lecture to be the sole event of a special plenary session of the meeting of the Nordic Assembly of Naturalists. Finally, the topic of Einstein's lecture, entitled "Fundamental Ideas and Problems of the Theory of Relativity," was unrelated to the scientific contribution for which Einstein was awarded the Nobel Prize.

Indeed, the official announcement of Einstein's prize went out of its way to disavow any consideration of relativity in the Swedish Academy's decision to reward Einstein's work. The cover letter that had accompanied his Nobel certificate specifically noted that he was being recognized for discovering the law of the photoelectric effect "without taking into account the value which will be accorded your relativity and gravitation theories after these are confirmed in the future."

Einstein received word that he had been awarded the Nobel Prize in October 1922, while his steamer was chugging toward a lecture tour in Japan. He had accepted the Japanese invitation to allow time for things to cool off back home in Berlin, where his friend Walther Rathenau recently had been assassinated and he had received death threats. Perhaps because he resented how long it had taken the Nobel assembly to recognize his contributions and because the members of the assembly appeared to be going out of their way to ignore his most important work, Einstein refused the invitation to backtrack to Sweden for the December 10 Nobel ceremony and dinner. He even stopped to lecture in Jerusalem and Spain on his way back to Berlin. Einstein's absence spoke volumes. However, just as the prophet Elijah seats himself in an unfilled chair for the Jewish Passover Seder, the spirit of the seer of theoretical physics inhabited the Nobel stage.

Had he been present in Stockholm that evening, he would have heard Professor Arrhenius declare at the outset of his introduction, "There is no physicist living today whose name has become so widely known as that of Albert Einstein." Arrhenius cited the theory of relativity and its philosophical ramifications as the main reason for Einstein's renown. Next, he gave due attention to Einstein's 1905 paper on Brownian motion, which he noted had given rise to the burgeoning field of colloid chemistry. Finally, he addressed the reason the physics committee had chosen Einstein to receive the prize: Einstein's discovery of the law of the photoelectric effect. In a feat of linguistic gymnastics, the committee had recommended Einstein—and the full Nobel assembly had approved him—not for the photoelectric effect itself, which Philipp Lenard showed to be the result of ultraviolet light striking a metal surface; and not for the finding that the energy of the electrons emitted was related to the frequency of the incident light; Lenard had described this as well. Einstein was being honored specifically for his law employing Planck's constant, which explicitly defined the relationship between the wavelength of the incident light and the energy released.

In the law of the photoelectric effect, Einstein had drawn together two important lines of inquiry in early-twentieth-century physics: quantum theory and photodynamics. Citing American Robert Millikan's elegant experimental proof of Einstein's theoretical triumph, Arrhenius concluded his introduction by noting, "Einstein's law has become the basis of quantitative photochemistry in the same way as Faraday's law is the basis of electrochemistry."

At the same time as Einstein was out to sea, Philipp Lenard was attending the 1922 meeting of the German Society of Natural Scientists and Physicians, the same society that had hosted his 1920 debate with Einstein. His face must have registered shock at the announcement made during an interlude in the scientific sessions. After all, he was the 1905 laureate. It is likely that he'd had some interchanges with certain physics committee members wherein there had been agreement that Einstein's theoretical ravings were inappropriate for Nobel Prize consideration. He had heard that committee member Allvar Gullstrand had privately told a mathematician friend that "Einstein must never receive a Prize even if the whole world demands it." Surely, the announcement had been in error. The awarding of a prize to Einstein was unacceptable, if only because it cheapened his own distinction.

Although he must have realized that any attempt to reverse the decision was hopeless, Lenard nonetheless whipped off a four-page letter to the Swedish Academy, datelined Heidelberg, January 23, 1923.

> Highly esteemed sirs,
> As a member of your academy and previous recipient of the Nobel Prize, I believe I should communicate the following thoughts regarding the awarding of the Nobel Prize to Mr. Einstein. It would seem a mistake to me to remain silent toward you as the relevant center. Experts in the field would consider this mistake to weigh even more heavily as they know that this award had vividly occupied me for a long time.

Lenard acknowledged that the Prize had rightly not been given for Einstein's well-known theories of gravitation or relativity but for "less contentious thoughts." He also conceded that Einstein's law of the photoelectric effect had been "at least partially verified." Still, he continued,

> I can, however, not appreciate the communication of thoughts without empiric testing—of thoughts that could just as well be right or wrong, of sheer hypotheses, as achievements of the natural sciences, even less so as there was no discovery or progress whatsoever, for which this prize originally had been meant . . . what could render these thoughts valuable would be their diligent examination based on empirical testing.

The last complaint ignored the work of Robert Millikan, cited by Professor Arrhenius in his Nobel introduction of Einstein, which anyone conversant in the field would find odd. Citing Einstein's 1905 article in *Annalen der Physik*, "On a Heuristic Point of View Concerning the Production and Transformation of Light," in which Einstein laid out his law, Lenard wrote,

[E]xperts in the fields and persons acquainted with the historical facts know that there is nothing new which is proven in this work and there is nothing proven which is new, either. In fact, they know that there is nothing new at all in it other than the assumption that the energy quanta of Mr. Planck are not so much energy elements but rather light quanta. . . . The hypothesis [of Einstein] is based on (1) Mr. Planck's observation of energy elements in 1901 . . . as well as (2) my own work on the nature of the photoelectric effect performed in 1899-1902 and a unique property of this effect observed at that time . . . (3) Stoke's rule, which had been known for longer, and (4) my discovery based on detailed studies of phosphorescence in 1904 that the induction of phosphorescence also constitutes a photoelectric effect.

Lenard concluded, "Mr. Einstein's work does not contain more than a summary of these previous works with a few hypothetical additions." Copying a page from his Nobel Lecture's dismissal of Roentgen's contributions to the discovery of X-rays as trivial, Lenard noted that "with the methods developed by myself, [Einstein] was able to demonstrate that Planck's energy quanta, in fact, play a role in the transformation of light energy—which was to be expected, as these elements mean something in reality . . . [Einstein's 1905] publication of a specific hypothesis had been unnecessary, as it had been clear from Planck's work that the role of energy elements had to follow this rule."

Having presented his case, Lenard then asked the key rhetorical questions, ones that echoed his long-term gripes about theoretical physics more generally: "Where is the scientific achievement in Mr. Einstein's publication? Is the uttering of thoughts that do not even need a mathematical work to create them, that create such dismal contradictions . . . really a deed of science? Or does it become one by the superfluous addition of mathematical equations?"

Lenard believed that he grasped the situation. The Nobel Prize given Einstein for his law of the photoelectric effect was "nothing more than a subterfuge that was taken to avoid too great a disgrace" by recognizing his relativity theory. He closed with the following:

I deeply and utterly regret that the Swedish Academy and the Nobel Committee have not summoned enough clear German spirit to evade a fraud like this. My regret is all the deeper as the public attention that is rightfully stirred by the granting of a Nobel Prize will lead to a further acceptance of these fraudulent theories. To do my part against this, I wish that my concerns be publicly known. May—after all the history of science—this erroneous notion not be further nourished, that the striving for human recognition and the lack of reverence for still undiscovered truths be an indicator of scientific spirit.

To the Academy and the Committees

Yours faithfully,

P. Lenard

The press caught wind of Lenard's letter. The conservative Swedish newspaper, *Nya Dagligt Allehande*, gave vent to Lenard's views, including his charge that Einstein was nothing more than a "publicity-seeking Jew." The rival *Svenska Dagbladet* condemned the explicit racism and ran an article on Lenard's anti-Einstein connections to the 1920 Working Society of German Scientists for the Preservation of Pure Science. In an ironic turnaround, an article published in *Svenska Dagbladet* chided Lenard for his failure to use "clear Germanic intellect."

Lenard's indignation was to be expected. Despite a clamor from scientists around the world, the traditionalists on the physics committee had prevented Einstein from receiving a Nobel Prize for a dozen years. His recognition for the law of the photoelectric effect came only after the deaths of two conservative physics committee members and the appointment to the committee of a politically savvy new member who was much more inclined toward—and knowledgeable about—the theoretical physics typified by Einstein's work. The Academy's resistance to Einstein made it look silly in the eyes of both scientists and the general public. Things had reached such a state that by the time Einstein received his Nobel Prize, the Nobel assembly more needed Einstein's acceptance of the prize to salvage its leaky reputation than Einstein required the Academy's benediction of his work.

Einstein had first been nominated for the Nobel Prize for physics in 1910. However, the same battle that raged in Germany between the old science of experimental physics and the new theoretical physics also consumed the attentions of Swedish scientists. Three of the five members of the Nobel physics committee were drawn from among the strongly conservative, experimental physicists of Uppsala University, an ancient and renowned seat of learning located in nearby Stockholm. Sometimes referred to as the "Small Popes in Uppsala" for the power they wielded and their certainty in their own views, Professors Per Gustaf David Granqvist, Allvar Gullstrand, and Clas Bernhard Hasselberg, often with the complicity of committee members Svante Arrhenius and Vilhelm Carlheim-Gyllensköld, managed to quash any award to Albert Einstein. During 1910–1922, the only Nobel Prizes awarded to theoretical physicists were the 1914 award to Max von Laue for his work on X-ray diffraction by crystals, and the 1918 award to Max Planck for quantum theory.

Nominations for Einstein came as regularly as the ticking of the clock in the Bern City Hall tower that had helped inspire his theory of relativity. Except for 1911 and 1915, he received nominations every year between 1910, when only a single German nominator submitted his name, and 1922, when seventeen esteemed scientists from around the world nominated him for the prize. His combined total of sixty-three nominations for 1910–1922 was far more than any other candidate ever received.

However, Einstein's candidacy presented several unique problems. An initial hurdle was that some committee members held that the theory of relativity was not actually physics at all, but that it fell into the realm of the theory of knowledge, or epistemology. Another was the argument that the theory of relativity had too little relevance to the real world of the senses. His critics on the committee adopted Philipp Lenard's argument that the theory did not conform to common sense. It was unclear how Einstein's theories stacked up against the importance of other contenders' work and whether, in accordance with Alfred Nobel's will, Einstein's theories actually benefited mankind.

However, the main objection of relativity naysayers was that the theory of relativity had insufficient empirical support. Although the theory had shown itself accurate in a small number of circumstances, it lacked proof of more general applicability.

In 1910, when the physics committee considered seventeen nominees, Einstein's name was put forward for the first time by the winner of the 1909 Nobel Prize for Chemistry, Wilhelm Ostwald, to whom Einstein had unsuccessfully applied for a job in 1905, when he had just received his doctoral degree. He and Ostwald had recently become personally acquainted during the granting of honorary degrees to both men in Geneva. Ostwald cited the far-reaching consequences of Einstein's theory of relativity as his rationale for nominating the young physicist, then only thirty-one years of age. "With this new principle's help," the committee acknowledged, "A number of previously difficult to understand phenomena obtain a simple interpretation. . . . Einstein has pointed to a whole lot of phenomena against which the principle may be tested. This is an indication of its radical significance." However, in concluding that there was insufficient empirical evidence to support Einstein's theory, the committee decided that "it is justified to wait for the result of such tests in some important cases before the principle is accepted and especially before it is rewarded with a Nobel Prize."

No nominations came for Einstein during 1911, when the Wuerzburg physicist Wilhelm Wien won the Nobel for physics, but there were four in 1912, three in 1913, and two in 1914. In these years, the committee routinely categorized nominations by their perceived type:

- New discoveries that help further understand or apply existing knowledge;
- New explanations of phenomena that help the evolution of theories;
- New methods or instruments that have the potential to improve quantitation;
- New measurements that helped to determine the accuracy of theories;
- New theories

Einstein's nominations most often fell within the last of these categories, which was *terra incognita* for the committee members. Like Lenard, the committee members saw relativity as alien to the world of sensory experience and, therefore, more of an intellectual exercise than meaningful science with practical applications. Because Alfred Nobel's will explicitly stated that the prize should be given for tangible benefits, Einstein had an uphill climb from the outset. In fact, by the end of the committee's deliberations for 1914, it was clear that it would be some time before Einstein would be seriously considered, if he would be at all. That year, they had dismissed his accomplishments with a single frigid sentence: "For the time being, there is no reason to take into account his candidacy."

The war years of 1914–1918 did little to improve Einstein's chances for a Nobel Prize. In addition to the prejudices of the physics committee, he now had to fight the Allies' perceptions of German scientists. He might be an atypical German, but in many eyes, he still was a German.

Einstein kept busy, putting the finishing touches on his theory of general relativity and extending his considerations to gravitation. In 1915, he conceived a series of lectures on relativity that he presented before the Prussian Academy of Sciences during November. The lectures provided a framework for him to organize his work and publish his new theory of general relativity comprehensively in an extensive article in the March 1916 issue of *Annalen der Physik*. He quickly followed up that publication with a short book entitled *Relativity—the Special and General Theory*, designed to explain his ideas to an educated general audience in plain language, with little math. Between 1915 and 1919, Einstein received fifteen nominations. Given the strong anti-German bias of most Europeans, these mostly originated from German scientists and physicists living in neutral countries. Among those nominating Einstein in 1919, surprisingly, was physics committee member Svante Arrhenius, the winner of the 1903 Prize.

Following his completion and publication of the theory of general relativity, Einstein published several articles intimating the cosmological ramifications of his theories that included the predictions that eventually secured his fame. There were three main cosmological events that Einstein addressed. The first was a relativity-based explanation of the shifting of the perihelion, or the closest point of Mercury's orbit relative to the sun. The Nobel committee acknowledged the workability of Einstein's solution but, in once again denying Einstein the Nobel Prize, their report noted that, so far, there had been no validation of the correctness of the other two proofs: Einstein's prediction that the sun's gravity would bend the light of closely aligned stars, and his assertion that the sun's gravity would cause a small shift in the red spectrum of the sun relative to the same part of the light spectrum on earth. The committee concluded, "There are also hitherto unobserved phenomena that have been derived from the theory [meaning the two predictions], and it seems obvious that it must be of fundamental significance when ascribing a value to it [the theory of relativity] whether or not the derived consequences agree with reality."

Thus, a prize for relativity was rejected in 1918, and again in 1919, at least in part on the grounds of insufficient empirical data in support of his theories. Ironically, when nominators proposed a prize for one or another of his accomplishments other than relativity, the committee found a new argument for why an award for anything other than relativity simply wouldn't do:

> [It] would appear peculiar to the learned world if Einstein were to receive the Prize precisely for the work just reviewed [meaning his contributions to science other than relativity], regardless of its obvious great value and utility for the development of science, and not for his other major papers which much more than the ones at hand have attracted the attention of those who have proposed him.

Even as scientific investigation chipped away at the objections to his candidacy, like a celestial body in Einstein's expanding universe, it seemed that the Nobel Prize was receding ever farther from his grasp.

Soon, however, events in warmer locales would change the Nobel equation. Early in November 1919, preliminary results of the British solar eclipse expedition leaked to Einstein's friends in Zurich. Another of Einstein's three key predictions was confirmed as accurate. The gravitational field of the sun did indeed bend starlight as it passed closely by its considerable mass. His friend, Edgar Meyer, sent Einstein a congratulatory poem on the back of a postcard:

> All doubt removed
> Finally, it is found
> That light bends naturally
> To Einstein's greater glory

In the event that the British results were upheld through their final analysis, Einstein would have ticked off yet another necessary criterion of what was proving to be a very demanding Nobel committee.

How things had arrived at this state was as much due to good fortune as detailed planning. Einstein's Dutch friend Willem de Sitter had passed to Arthur Eddington at Cambridge the cosmological articles published by Einstein during the war. Even before he was aware of Einstein's celestial predictions, Eddington had been considering an expedition to conduct experiments during the May 29, 1919, total solar eclipse. The Einstein papers increased his enthusiasm for the venture.

To improve his chances of success, Eddington planned on conducting his work at two sites. Along with his assistant, E. T. Cottingham, he traveled to Principe Island in the Bay of Guinea, off the coast of West Africa. The other party was led by Andrew Crommelin and Charles Davidson, who set up shop near Fortaleza, Brazil. Both locations would have a few minutes when the eclipse was complete to photograph the position of nearby stars in the darkened sky.

On November 6, 1919, in a joint meeting of the Royal Society of London and the Royal Astronomical Society, the retired Cambridge professor and Nobel laureate, J. J. Thompson, announced the salient result. The photographic data obtained during the eclipse showed a deflection of 1.7 degrees in the position of relevant stars relative to where they were positioned in the night sky when the sun was not adjacent to them. It was exactly what Einstein had predicted and double the deflection expected on the basis of classical Newtonian physics. The positive outcome was run in the *Times of London* and then throughout the world. Einstein was the new Newton! The new Copernicus! Surely, the press speculated, the Nobel physics committee would see a way to vote Einstein a Nobel Prize.

Einstein's new celebrity put him in something of a bind. One outcome of World War I was the isolation of German scientists, who were not welcome at meetings held elsewhere in Europe, a situation that did not begin to officially change until 1926. Einstein, however, was treated differently. Perhaps because he had spurned German nationalism, he became a favored nominee for the physics prize even for scientists from such countries as France, England, and the United States. In Germany, however, he became a lightning rod for right-wing extremists, who regarded his wartime behavior as un-German. This was the period that gave rise to Weyland's Working Group for the Preservation of Pure Science and its anti-relativity lecture series, the attacks of Ernst Gehrcke, and Lenard's radicalization. Communist factions, on the other hand, viewed Einstein's ideas of non-absolute time and relativistic motion as degenerate Western idealism, inappropriate for the reigning Soviet dialectic.

Einstein's international fame translated into more travel and more lectures, which he undertook not only as a scientist but also as an emissary of pacifism. During 1921, Einstein made his first trip to the United States in the company of Chaim Weitzmann, who had arranged a lecture tour to raise money for a Jewish university in Palestine. In New York, Einstein was feted with a ticker tape parade. He received the Barnard Medal for Meritorious Service to Science from the National Academy of Sciences and Columbia University. Americans loved the quirky European, and he lectured before huge crowds. At one particularly overcrowded event at Princeton University, Einstein is said to have turned to his host and marveled, "I never realized that so many Americans were interested in tensor analysis."

Einstein's participation in the Zionist-sponsored lecture tour conflicted with his ethos of anti-nationalism. However, Einstein was convinced of the rightness of his participation by Europe's increasingly virulent anti-Semitism and his burgeoning consciousness of his own ethnic heritage. Einstein, who, to this point in time had described himself as "the child of Jewish parents" and shown little affinity for any form of religion—he who had vocally eschewed nationalism—became a Zionist. All of this made him much more a man of the world than a man of Germany. A beleaguered postwar Germany took notice. He became a prominent target for reactionary critics, who referred to Einstein as "un-German" or "internationalist," a code word meant to brand Einstein with communist leanings.

Einstein received eight Nobel nominations in 1920, fourteen in 1921. Despite continuing hard feelings over the war, many of the nominations came from countries that had been Germany's enemies. The large number of nominations reflected the general excitement over Eddington's findings. In his 1921 nomination, Eddington called Einstein's theory of general relativity "one of the greatest landmarks in the history of scientific thought." His theory provided the first fresh insights on gravitation since Newton, conjoined into a single theory an explanation for the workings of numerous important natural phenomena, reconciled science and philosophy, and enabled further development by other scientists.

In light of the Eddington results, the Nobel physics committee charged Svante Arrhenius with drafting a special report on Einstein and relativity in 1920 and Allvar Gullstrand with drafting one in 1921. Neither man had the background or worldview to understand the mathematics of Einstein's theories and the ramifications of his vision. As a result, both reports clearly favored the views of the experimentalists in expressing skepticism about particulars of Einstein's theories. Arrhenius swallowed whole Gehrcke's charges of plagiarism regarding Einstein's explanation of the shift in the perihelion of Mercury. He seized upon uncertainties in Eddington's measurements.

If possible, Gullstrand was even harder on Einstein than Arrhenius. His evaluation determined that relativity theory "has the character of an article of faith rather than a scientific hypothesis. . . . The effects [predicted by relativity theory] are so small that they lay under the margin of observational error." He dismissed Einstein's explanation of the perihelion of Mercury as circular reasoning. He leapt upon irregularities in Eddington's processes and data, declaring the work completely unreliable.

Chief among the Small Popes, Gullstrand was the individual who most firmly stood between Einstein and a Nobel Prize, though other committee members were also resistant. Hasselberg, who had taken ill during the 1921 proceedings, concurred with Gullstrand in saying, "It is highly improbable that Nobel considered speculations such as these [meaning the theory of relativity] to be the object of his prizes."

If not for the deaths of two of the Small Popes, it is unlikely that anything would have changed. The demise of Hasselberg and Granqvist paved the way for the appointment of Carl Wilhelm Oseen, first as a temporary consulting committee member and later as a permanent member. Oseen was a mathematician and theoretical physicist whose principle interest was hydrodynamics. A member of the faculty at Uppsala, his worldview was nonetheless contrary to the pre-relativistic experimentalism of the other Uppsala professors on the committee. Gullstrand had frequently sought Oseen's advice while working on his 1921 evaluation of Einstein, but each time Oseen allayed one of Gullstrand's concerns, the elder scientist seized upon another. In the end, Gullstrand's report echoed the chief concern expressed by Philipp Lenard: Einstein's theories were abstractions, ungrounded in reality. On that basis, the theory of relativity was belief, not science.

Oseen's election to the Swedish Academy of Sciences and his subsequent appointment to the Nobel physics committee changed everything. He was a new and demanding force. Oseen had nominated Einstein for the prize in 1920 and 1921. Seeing that a prize for relativity was impossible, he struck upon the idea of proposing an award for Einstein's discovery of the law of the photoelectric effect. Now a member of the physics committee, Oseen managed in the November 1921 committee meeting to fight off a comment in the Arrhenius evaluation that it would seem odd to ignore Einstein's theory of relativity by awarding him a prize for lesser known work. Oseen forced a stalemate in the discussion; the committee recommended that the 1921 prize be reserved for future determination. Although the full Nobel assembly upheld this result, a number of voices raised the issue of Einstein. When would the committee get around to nominating the most popular scientist of this, or perhaps any, era?

Seventeen nominators supported Einstein in the committee's November 1922 deliberations. Although most of the nominations were for relativity theory, there was a fair sampling of letters backing Einstein's work on Brownian motion and the photoelectric effect. Oseen wrote an indepth report citing why he felt Einstein's law of the photoelectric effect was a significant enough contribution to warrant a Nobel Prize. In his report, he linked Einstein's law to Niels Bohr's atomic model. Oseen was a close friend of the young Dane. He admired Bohr's model of electrons whizzing at different energy levels around a central nucleus, calling it "the most beautiful of all the beautiful" concepts in contemporary theoretical physics. Oseen showed how Einstein's law underpinned understanding of Bohr's model and how drawing both together sustained Planck's quantum theory, which previously had stood apart in physics. Toward the end of his report, Oseen summarized his argument for Einstein:

> Einstein, with his daring law, had hit the nail on the head. . . . Almost all confirmation of Bohr's theory, and with it, all spectroscopic confirmations, are at the same time confirmations of Einstein's law. . . . The Einsteinian proposition and Bohr's contentwise identical frequency conditions are currently one of the most certain laws that obtain in physics. . . . The greatest significance, and equally the most convincing confirmation Einstein's proposition has received is by virtue of it being one of the prerequisite conditions on which Bohr built his atomic theory. Almost all confirmations of Bohr's atomic theory are equally confirmations of Einstein's proposition. . . . The discovery of Einstein's law is without any doubt one of the most significant events in the history of physics.

Finally, at the very end, so there would be no doubt where he stood, Oseen gilded the lily. "Its discovery to me appears to fully deserve a Nobel Prize in physics."

Oseen's mastery of mathematics and theoretical physics silenced Gullstrand, who most vigorously opposed Einstein receiving the prize. Arrhenius was won over by the idea that choosing Einstein might not only address the public mockery of the Academy but also aid the process of renewing international scientific relations. Oseen capitalized on the situation by proposing that the committee support Einstein for the reserved 1921 Prize and Bohr for 1922.

Gullstrand's consolation was the 1923 Prize for the experimentalist Robert Millikan, whose exhaustive investigations had proven the accuracy of Einstein's law. Admonishing the Lenard-led reactionaries who persisted in their senseless attacks on theoretical physics, Millikan acknowledged the reciprocal debt that theory and experiment owed, each to the other:

> The fact [is] that science walks forward on two feet, namely theory and experiment. . . . Sometimes it is one foot that is put forward first, sometimes the other, but continuous progress is only made by the use of both—by theorizing and then testing, or by finding new relations in the process of experimenting and then bringing the theoretical foot up and pushing it on beyond, and so on in unending alterations.

The physics committee's nomination of Einstein to the Nobel assembly was a welcome one, allaying, as it did, broader concerns about what effect the failure to recognize Einstein with a Nobel Prize was having on the reputation of the award. The announcement of Einstein's award was well received in many quarters. Worldwide, Einstein was a popular figure whose frequent appearances on the international lecture circuit were helping normalize scientific relationships among the countries that had opposed Germany in the Great War.

Lenard seethed, as did other reactionaries who promoted the notion that, despite his birth in Ulm, Einstein was not truly German. Paul Weyland, the demagogue who had conspired with Lenard and others to bring down Einstein at the Berlin Philharmonic lectures two years previously, traveled to Sweden just prior to Einstein's Nobel Lecture in an unsuccessful effort to mobilize dissent.

The machinations of the Nobel physics committee lay in the past that warm day in Gothenburg in 1923 when, before an engaged audience,

Einstein launched into his Nobel Lecture. It was a day that bore witness to the accomplishments of a unique life. There would be many such days during the next ten years. Yet all the while, the potential for trouble was mounting. Back home in Berlin, a backlash was brewing against Einstein's activities during the war, his opposition to German nationalism, and his support of the Weimar government. Germany was experiencing a rise in reactionary fervor. At the root of it all were the Nazi Party and its "Fuehrer," Adolf Hitler. The Lenards and Weylands, the Goebbels, the Speers, and the Himmlers would soon have their day. Fingers were being pointed. Einstein would not escape their notice.

9

DANGEROUS CHOICES

At 8:30 on the evening of November 8, 1923, a pistol shot rang out in Munich's Buegerbrauekeller beer hall, followed closely by a shout of "Silence!" The overflow crowd of more than three thousand anxiously complied. They had been listening to Commissioner Gustav von Kahr, the chief official representing Germany's Weimar government in Bavaria. He had been in the midst of outlining his plans to implement his newly conferred state-of-emergency powers to quell the violent civil unrest plaguing the city. As Kahr stepped away from the podium, the throng turned as one to the source of the interruption. Backed by six hundred armed SA storm troopers filing into the main hall, Adolf Hitler, Erich Ludendorff, and Hermann Goering pushed their way through the throng.

"The national revolution has begun," Hitler announced. "No one may leave the hall. . . . The Bavarian and Reich governments have been replaced and a provisional national government has been formed. The barracks of the *Reichswehr* [the army] and police are occupied. The army and the police are marching on the city under the Swastika banner."

None of this was true, but the stunned crowd was in no position to doubt or to argue. Hitler spirited von Kahr and two of his lieutenants, Lieutenant General Otto Herrmann von Lossow and Police Chief Hans Ritter von Seisser, into a back room, where he threatened the men with his pistol in an effort to get them to agree to join his revolution. When the Weimar officials declined, as a compromise, Hitler accepted their oath that the three men would not actively oppose the NSDAP. Immediately following their release, they all reneged.

Hitler then returned to the main hall. Giving the impression that von Kahr had agreed to switch sides, he announced, "The [Weimar] government of the November criminals and the Reich President are declared to be removed. A new national government will be named this very day in Munich. A new German National Army will be formed immediately. . . . The task of the provisional German National Government is to organize the march on that sinful Babel, Berlin, and save the German people! Tomorrow will find either a National Government in Germany or us dead!"

In fact, neither event occurred. The ensuing comedy of errors, reminiscent of a Keystone Cops film, ended ignominiously. During an effort to take over the Bavarian Defense Ministry the following morning, Hitler's attempt to oust the government and name himself "Fuehrer" failed. Goering was shot in the groin. Hitler suffered a dislocated shoulder when the man with whom he had linked arms in solidarity dropped to the ground and pulled Hitler down with him. Hitler's life was saved by his bodyguard, who threw himself upon Germany's future leader and absorbed several fatal bullets. In all, sixteen *Putschists*, four police officers, and a bystander were killed during the brief revolt.

Afterward, the Nazis scattered. Some of the leaders of the *Putsch* were arrested, while others, including Rudolf Hess, Hermann Goering, and Ernst Hanfstaengl, escaped to Austria. Hitler hid in the attic of Hanfstaengl's country house on the Staffelsee for two nights before being arrested the morning of the third day following the debacle. Hitler blamed the failure of the *Putsch* on von Kahr, and while he was in no position to retaliate then, he certainly did not forget. Eleven years later, on June 30, 1934—the "Night of the Long Knives"—the Nazis eliminated their political competition, and Hitler settled his score with von Kahr. Two SS officers arrested von Kahr in his Munich apartment. They severely abused and beat him on his way to the concentration camp in Dachau, where, on the order of the camp commandant, Theodor Eicke, he was shot to death.

Following Hitler's arrest, he spent a fretful night in jail, certain he would be summarily executed before daybreak. His spirits improved when he was told he would receive a public trial in the People's Court. He would use the opportunity—and this stage—to good advantage. By turning the proceedings into an indictment of the Weimar government, he secured a notorious living martyrdom that would serve him well when he sought to revive his political career. Politically sympathetic judges gave him a sentence of five years of imprisonment in Landsberg Fortress—the least onerous among the possible punishments for high treason. The court later commuted his sentence after he had served just nine months with the proviso that he refrain from speechmaking for at least several years. During his time in prison, Hitler wrote his autobiography, *Mein Kampf,* a rambling anti-Semitic, anti-Marxist diatribe that detailed his strategy for the ascent of the Nazis to ultimate political power.

For Philipp Lenard, Hitler's beer hall *Putsch* was galvanizing. He felt impelled to express his boundless admiration for the man who he believed had sacrificed so much for the cause of the German people. In his 1924 publication, "The Hitler Spirit and Science," Lenard managed to combine his hero worship for Hitler with his antipathy for the Jewish physicists who had come to dominate German science. Written with Johannes Stark, the article was formatted as an open letter to Germany's newspapers and received wide distribution. Comparing Hitler's integrity and dedication to the great scientists of the past, the authors wrote,

> That spirit of total clarity, of honesty towards the outer world and at the same time inner uniformity, that spirit which hates any compromising activity because it is insincere. But we have already recognized . . . this spirit in the great scientists of the past: in Galileo, Kepler, Newton, and Faraday. We admire and revere it in the same way also in Hitler, Ludendorff, Poehner (the leaders of the Munich revolt) and their comrades. . . . Consider what it means to be privileged to have this kind of genius living among us in the flesh. . . . Experience reveals that the incarnations of this spirit are only of Aryan-German blood. . . . But it is also much better that the "man of the people" is doing it. He is here.

He has revealed himself as the Fuehrer of the sincere. We shall follow him.

The publication of "The Hitler Spirit and Science" was a watershed in Lenard's public expression of explicit anti-Semitic views. Lenard had, for the most part, kept his peace in reacting to Einstein's response to the lectures at the Berlin Philharmonic and at the *Einsteindebatte* at Bad Nauheim. Even for several years thereafter, Lenard had been cautious about openly engaging in anti-Semitic remarks. However, with the decline in his financial circumstances and embittered by the death of his son from kidney failure, Lenard assumed a more aggressive stance against Jewish involvement in German science. Comparing the existential Jewish threat to the essential German-Aryan character with the terminal events of the Greek and Roman civilizations, Lenard and Stark went on to warn their readers,

> But blood can also die out. . . . The exact same force is at work, always with the same Asian people behind it that brought Christ to the cross, Jordanus Brunus to the stake, and that shoots at Hitler and Ludendorff with machine guns and confines them within fortress walls. It is the fight of the dark spirits against the torchbearers. . . . Universities and their students have failed most of all precisely in those subjects for which they should have set the pace long ago.

Lenard's devolution toward open anti-Semitism advanced dramatically in response to two related incidents that occurred in June 1922. On June 24, a car pulled up to the vehicle carrying the German foreign minister, Walther Rathenau, and men opened fire, killing the car's occupants. The Weimar leadership ordered German flags to be flown at half-mast on June 27 and declared a national holiday of mourning. Lenard refused to obey the government edict. Rathenau was a liberal, a Jew, and a friend of Einstein, as well as a member of the despised Weimar government. The German flag atop the Heidelberg Institute of Physics flew proudly at full salute.

What happened next is a matter of perspective. Lodging a grievance with Lenard, a group of students from the university's socialist league and a number of the Institute's workers sought to discuss with Lenard what they viewed as his dishonoring of one of their heroes. Lenard's refusal to enter into a discourse with the group led to what Lenard later referred to as "the dangerous raid." There are several versions of what transpired; however, all accounts agree that Lenard suffered considerable psychic trauma. The June 30, 1922, edition of *Neue Zurcher Zeitung* offered the following lighthearted account of a dangerous situation that could easily have become violent:

Most amusing was the scene that caused both terror and laughter for the people of Heidelberg. Professor Lenard [is] one of the finest physicists of Germany, famous for his political squibs that he distributes among his most excellent colleagues. Born as a Hungarian (many say as a Jew), he is all the more a German nationalist. . . . A deployment of workers came across the New Bridge [of Heidelberg University] around 6 PM. They noticed what they had already expected [that the flag was not at half mast and that physics seminars had not been canceled]. At the same time, the Free Union of Students complained to the Rector of the University. . . . Four policemen climbed the stairs to request [compliance with the Ministry of Culture recommendations, but Lenard] shut the door in their face.

Then, the workers united [in front of the institute] and intended to use force. At the same time, nationalist students [in support of Lenard] aimed four water cannons at the crowd from above, and—unfortunately—large rocks also were thrown, which had obviously had been prepared beforehand. Only now did the workers seize the laboratory. The female students took flight. The men grabbed the professor and forced the police to lead him in a jeering deployment across the bridge to the student union house.

A large crowd formed and debated the issues. The district attorney arrived and tried to deescalate the situation. . . . After an hour, a police officer announced from the balcony that the professor would be taken into custody for his own protection. . . . "There will be a car in a moment. . . ." The crowd objected. There were cries of "He shall walk! We also need to walk to the jail! No car!" [An ombudsman announced] "The man will walk, but you shall do nothing to him. I have vouched my life for this!" [There was] thundering laughter. After a while an alleyway formed through the crowd. . . . [One could see] the plaintiveness of this stumbling man in more detail, how he was brought to safety trembling. All held true to their promise: . . . the police did everything to keep the peace; the workers were full of discipline. When their prisoner walked through the crowd, they laughed.

Resentful of his treatment at the hands of the mob and chastened by near death, he immersed himself in the speeches of Adolf Hitler and the writings of Houston Stewart Chamberlain exalting the Aryan race. Lenard was fully radicalized. He expressed his new worldview in a 1922 address at the University of Heidelberg, wherein he likened the activities of the Weimar government to the superstitious practices of the Middle Ages:

What is not consistent with reality can never affect people other than negatively. We should not be fooled to think that back then was the dark Middle Ages and now we live in enlightened, bright modern times. Today it is exactly as dark and dangerous, in fact darker and more dangerous, to announce a new knowledge and again precisely that knowledge, which is most important for men to know, as this knowledge provides the highest enlightenment in regard to the things around us and how these affect us. Today there are other powers, which prevent us from saying what is good for men and what not; however, it is exactly as dark as at the time of the witch trials or witch belief. Or is it more reasonable than witch processes, if you govern a people from a perspective, that this people bears the guilt for a war, which it has not caused? That is even darker than any witch belief; thus, there is no great difference between those times and today.

Professionally, Lenard became further entrenched in the science of the past. In his opposition to theoretical physics, he gave no quarter to any aspect of relativity. He gave no more credence to special relativity, the tenets of which he formerly had accepted, than he did general relativity. All that was needed was a proper venue for him to publicly express his philosophy. A perfectly suitable one was fast approaching. He began his preparations for the hundredth anniversary meeting of the same Society of German Scientists and Physicians that had met in Bad Nauheim two years earlier. The upcoming conference was scheduled for Leipzig in the fall of 1922. The meeting was an especially important one because German scientists were still not welcomed at conferences elsewhere in Europe and some were actively dissuaded from attending.

Still hoping to sway his colleagues away from Einstein's theories, Lenard reconsidered his thoughts on ether, setting down his views in his 1922 edition of *Ether and Urether*. He proposed the existence of two ethers, both derived from previous models, to explain the observed physical phenomena. In this construct, every atom had its own ether, the amount of which varied according to the state of the atom. Lenard referred to this ether as "the ether of matter," because each particle of matter could emit or absorb portions of its surrounding ether. The other ether, which Lenard termed "the urether," he considered "the ether of space." The urether was the medium that facilitated the passage of electromagnetic radiation at the speed of light, free of the burden of matter.

In the introduction to this revised edition of *Ether and Urether*, entitled "Exhortation to German Naturalists," Lenard revisited a gripe he had leveled at Einstein in the past. He claimed that Einstein's false promotion of his unproven theories was indicative of his poor character, and he charged the Society of German Scientists and Physicians with complicity. "It makes a difference," he wrote, "whether mischief carries on only in the newspapers, or whether the Society, from which one expects a clear, elegantly balanced opinion, participated in this nonsense. . . . Much more disastrous still . . . [is] the concealed conceptual confusion which floats about Einstein as a 'German' scientist."

In a remarkable demonstration of psychological projection, Lenard continued,

> It is a well-known Jewish feature to quite immediately bring factual matters into the realm of personal disputes. . . ." The healthy German spirit . . . must deflect from itself the foreign spirit [of Judaism] which arises as a dark power everywhere and which is so clearly designated

in everything that belongs to the theory of relativity. We live in no less a dark age than the Inquisition. . . . I want the German naturalists to make clearer sense, proving their worth to me by bringing the enlightenment to break the power of the dark spirit everywhere possible.

In this regard, Lenard was perpetually disappointed. Not only did his colleagues ignore the looming threat but also they objected strongly to his racial references. Years later, he wrote in the margins of the introduction to his copy of *Ether and Urether*, "The German naturalists of that time, indeed all of the university professors, were not of assistance. Only Adolf Hitler gave a basis eleven years later for breaking the power of the dark spirit even in science through his Third Reich."

Leading up to the conference, Lenard and others attempted to provide experimental proof of ether, with its new duality, but their efforts were in vain. Regardless, Lenard was not dissuaded. His Heidelberg speech foreshadowed the arguments he planned for Einstein at Leipzig:

> Now, Einstein says: I assume, that ether does not exist at all. If we don't wish to see ether, space and heaven must be empty. Nothing should be between heaven and earth, only sordid matter, nothing else for natural scientists to encounter. This is assumed by the very same man [Einstein]. I have to present him here as a whole, because I consider it not right that one can and should distinguish between the man and the researcher, as both are coming from the same depth.

Lenard's tone here is mocking. How is it even remotely possible that the universe could operate in the absence of at least one ether? Ridiculous, but especially so coming from a man who lives on the edge of sedition.

> Thus I talk of this Mr. Einstein, who brings us [his concern for] Eastern Jews in the tens of thousands . . . while the same man, who has a very special relationship with those people who had been recognized in war times as traitors of the patrimony and who had been thrown out of the country or had been hanged. So, with this man the spaces of the sky are empty.

In the same presentation, Lenard reestablished one of his earlier objections to Einstein's theories:

> I am a friend of simple thinking, which has led to the greatest successes of natural scientists at all times. From the most simple thoughts have always arisen the greatest successes, in the most varied areas. Has Bismarck's thinking been any different from simple? . . . The simple mind is a great German characteristic.

Thus, as he had asserted two years earlier at Bad Nauheim, the theory of relativity had an "exaggerated nature." It failed the test of common sense. It was nothing more than a "hypothesis heap."

Lenard expected to confront Einstein directly at Leipzig, as he had at Bad Nauheim during the 1920 conference. In this, he was disappointed. Einstein had been scheduled to present his latest considerations on relativity, but anxious colleagues convinced him to withdraw. The spread of open anti-Semitism among elements of the gathering, the threat that Lenard might be distributing his anti-relativity pamphlets, and that Einstein's name had recently begun to appear on "death lists" offering a bounty for his assassination all spoke to the wisdom of canceling. It was too bad, in a way. Had he been there, he would have had the satisfaction of seeing Lenard's consternation upon the announcement of Einstein having been selected to receive the 1921 Nobel Prize, which the Nobel Academy had reserved from the previous year. Instead, Einstein was on a steamship making its way toward a lecture tour he had hastily arranged in Japan.

For Lenard, Einstein's Nobel Prize was the final straw. Sixty years of age, seemingly outmaneuvered by Einstein at every turn, and feeling increasingly isolated, with his most creative years as a scientist behind him and his colleagues deserting experimental physics for the empty promise of relativity, there was nothing for him to do but to support the National Socialist German Workers Party. Nazi rhetoric promised a new world order, one that would not tolerate the dark ravings of the relativity Jew.

Following the Leipzig conference, Lenard mostly stepped away from serious science, dedicating himself to reactionary politics. He further personalized his anti-Jewish fervor. Einstein was the living personification of the depraved Jewish spirit that had insinuated itself into German science. At his Heidelberg presentation in the spring of 1922, Lenard had declaimed, "At the end I want to tell you that I hope that you will not think of me as an adversary of Einstein, as sometimes is stated. I am far from it, as this would be much too little. It would be too low a goal."

What Lenard wished for was not simply the defeat of his old foe but the complete erasure of Einstein's ideas, writings, and pronouncements—a blank slate, as though Einstein had never been born.

10

LENARD AND HITLER

On the afternoon of March 23, 1933, less than two months after President Paul von Hindenberg had appointed him Chancellor of the Weimar Republic, Adolf Hitler sat amid the members of Germany's parliament, the Reichstag. He appeared to listen thoughtfully as the Social Democrat leader Otto Wel implored the Reichstag to vote down the Enabling Act proposed by Hitler's right-wing coalition.

Hitler realized that being in this place, at this time, put him on the cusp of a historic moment. He had begun his political ascent as the head of propaganda of the ultra-nationalist German Workers Party. In 1920, he assumed leadership and renamed the organization the National Socialist German Workers Party. For much of the next decade, the party's fortunes rose and fell inversely with the economy. But as the icy grip of the worldwide depression took hold in 1929, and unemployment became epidemic, the Nazis' scapegoating of socialists, communists, and Jews for the general misery gained currency among the populace. Party membership soared.

Despite his apparent calm, Hitler's brain was racing ahead to when he would take the podium. He had thoroughly prepared himself for what he expected would be the defining speech of his political career. In effect, the passage of the Enabling Act would give Chancellor Hitler and his cabinet absolute dictatorial powers to pass decrees without Reichstag approval or the meddling of the aged president.

Wel finished with an impassioned plea for German honor. German honor! If only the Social Democrats had thought about German honor during the past fifteen years of kowtowing to the crippling demands of the armistice. If only they had rejected the myth foisted upon the public that Germany had been responsible for the Great War. They'd had their day, one that had lasted far too long. The time was ripe for revolution. Hitler was confident that he had just listened to the last embarrassingly mewling Reichstag speech he would ever have to hear.

When the crowd quieted, Hitler rose and made his way to the podium. Attired in a dark khaki combat uniform, a white armband bearing the Nazi swastika prominently encircling his left arm, he paused for a moment to collect his thoughts. Germany's parliament had assembled that day in the main chamber of Berlin's Kroll Opera House, because a month earlier the Reichstag building had mysteriously burned to the ground. It had clearly been arson, but the persons who set the fire remained at large. For the Nazis, the crime had been a godsend. The razing of the Reichstag had provided Chancellor Hitler with a pretext for his subsequent actions. Characterizing the fire as a communist plot, Hitler declared emergency powers, suspending individual rights in the name of public safety. To many, it all seemed too neat, as though it had been the Nazis who actually had ignited the blaze.

With new elections scheduled for March 5, Hitler unleashed his SA storm troopers into the streets to disrupt the activities of competing political factions. The brief campaign was among the most brutal in history. Nationalist reactionary factions, communists, and centrists battled openly in the streets while police looked the other way. Despite the rampant violence and unprecedented voter intimidation, the elections left the Nazis and their coalition of like-minded parties just short of a clear majority.

Hitler was not concerned about the electoral shortfall. He had thoroughly prepared for this moment. Nothing had been left to chance. Surveying the members of the Reichstag who were present that afternoon, he felt good about the Enabling Act's chances for success. There was more than the usual number of empty seats. His storm troopers, who now surrounded the Opera to ensure there would be no interruptions, had rounded up the worker-backed communist members and many of the more outspoken Social Democrats. Many of these individuals would soon become guests of the Reich. They were destined to experience the grim hospitality of the newly built Dachau concentration camp. It would be the first of a number of such facilities intended to silence Nazi opposition.

Starting slowly and calmly, Hitler began his address:

> Ladies and Gentlemen of the German Reichstag! By agreement with the Reich Government, today the National Socialist German Workers Party and the German National Peoples Party have presented to you for resolution a notice of motion concerning a "Law for Removing the Distress of Volk and Reich (the Enabling Act)." The reasons for this extraordinary measure are as follows: In November 1918, the Marxist organizations seized the executive power by means of a Revolution. Thus a breach of the Constitution was committed. . . . They sought moral justification by asserting that Germany or its government bore the guilt for the outbreak of the War.

His voice grew stronger and more emphatic as he denied Germany's culpability for the Great War. He reeled off the crimes of the Weimar government, which he noted had caused "the severest oppression of the entire German *Volk*." Spittle flew from his lips. His hands ticked off the reasons why the Reichstag must pass the Enabling Act, among them the mistreatment of ethnically German peoples living beyond Germany's armistice-constricted borders and the impact of the egregious reparations demanded by the Allies as part of the Treaty of Versailles. Near the end, Hitler got to his "ask":

> It would be inconsistent with the aim of the [Nazi-led] national uprising, and it would fail to suffice for the intended goal if the Government were to negotiate with and request the approval of the Reichstag for its measures in each given case.
>
> The Reich Government views a further session of the Reichstag as an impossibility under the present condition of a far-reaching state of excitation in the nation.

The outcome was never in doubt. The Reichstag, in essence, voted to relinquish authority and disband itself by the count of 491 to 94 in favor of the Enabling Act. The act, followed by the death of Hindenberg the next year, left Hitler with a clear path to cementing his victory by doing away with those he saw as his enemies, primarily Jews and communists. By the end of 1933, thirty thousand German citizens would be in government custody for "political crimes."

Hitler's ascent to Fuehrer of the Third Reich provided Philipp Lenard entrée into the most powerful halls of government. The Nazi party recognized Lenard to be an "Old Fighter," among those who had joined the party prior to Hitler assuming power. Lenard's speeches and writings evidenced his adoption of a reactionary philosophy that drove him toward the Nazi party as early as 1922. Beginning around that time, he'd begun to establish friendly personal relationships with a number of party leaders, including Hitler himself. Over the next several years, he became a familiar of Goebbels, Hess, and others among the Nazi leadership. Hitler wrote Lenard several very deferential personal letters, courting Lenard's involvement in party activities. On October 23, 1926, Hitler wrote,

> Highly esteemed professor!
> Your amiable letter reached me late as I was away from Munich. Thank you very much indeed. On October 2nd or 3rd I was unable to be in Karlsruhe, because the government of Baden prevented me from participating in any form [as part of the deal that released Hitler from serving his full sentence in prison]. I do sincerely hope that a conversation may be possible at another opportunity.

Hitler concluded the letter "With German Greetings," which Lenard would certainly have recognized as a point of collegiality based on racial distinction.

After a 1927 donation of 100 marks, Lenard received a letter from Hitler, who was "grateful [for the] donation for the family of the killed in action Hirschmann and for the wounded. I want to thank you in their name as well as in the name of the movement." Hitler's reference to Georg Hirschmann confirms Lenard's sympathies with and perhaps, by that time, membership in the party. Hirschmann was a shoemaker and a member of the Munich SA. He had led a group of fellow brown shirts in attacking a small street gathering of a rival political faction and had been clubbed in the head by a teenager named Karl Schott. He died the following day. At Hirschmann's funeral, Hitler martyred the dead man as the fifth Nazi to die in action in 1927. He then employed the "us versus them" tactic that would become a staple of his popular speeches, promising that the political violence against the Nazi movement ensured Hirschmann's would not be the last death they would mourn. To be a Nazi was to be oppressed but in the right. Despite the danger, the party would fight on.

By the time Hitler wrote Lenard in April 1929, he had become very direct in his efforts to recruit Lenard to the cause. "Much to my regret, I have heard that you visited the office and did not meet me," Hitler wrote. "I would be delighted to welcome you personally another time, soon. Maybe it would be possible for you to come to Nuremberg for the party convention."

What Hitler saw in Lenard were several qualities that he must have coveted. Despite the fact that his National Socialist German Workers Party had grown enormously in popular support since he had joined the party in 1920, it was still viewed by many potential voters as too extreme. Hitler would have perceived Lenard's reputation as a Nobel Prize–winning scientist as attractive in improving the Nazis' image and helping to convert more moderate Germans to his cause. Moreover, Hitler recognized in Lenard's feud with Einstein evidence that Lenard was a true believer. They saw eye-to-eye on the dangers of Jewish encroachment into German culture.

Finally, it wasn't just Lenard whom Hitler was recruiting. Along with Lenard came Einstein. Very early in his political development, Hitler hit upon the Jews as a scapegoat for what ailed the German people. However, he recognized he had a problem. It was hard to demonize an entire race in the abstract. He needed concrete examples. The liberal, internationalist, and, most importantly, Jewish Einstein was exactly the right whipping boy to further his party's popularity among an increasingly angry and xenophobic German electorate.

Lenard was sixty-one years old in 1933, when Hitler consolidated his power. Despite his age, he had lost little of his passion for his concerns about the threat to German culture posed by Einstein and the Jewish spirit. Nonetheless, he recognized that time would eventually slow him down. He increasingly involved his younger acolyte, Johannes Stark, in collaborations designed to achieve his ends. Lenard and Stark were well matched. If it were possible, Stark held even more extreme reactionary scientific and anti-Semitic views.

Born in a remote part of Bavaria to well-to-do parents, Stark was an academic *wunderkind*, achieving his doctoral degree at age twenty-three from the University of Munich. After six years as an assistant at Goettingen and a brief stint at the University of Hanover, he was appointed professor at the University of Aachen in 1909. At this time, he was considered, along with Einstein, to be a leading proponent of quantum theory. By 1912, however, his quarrelsome nature began to get him into trouble. A former colleague at Goettingen, Nobelist James Franck, said of Stark, "He was a pain in the neck in every aspect. However, I have to admit he had good ideas. And early on, he had this idea that photochemistry was a quantum process. Not as clearly as Einstein, but nevertheless, he had it."

Beginning in 1912, Stark engaged in a series of quarrels with Einstein over his perception that Einstein was usurping credit for discoveries that was rightfully his. Over similar concerns, he also alienated the politically powerful Arnold Sommerfeld, who had supported him for the Aachen position.

Stark's dispute with Sommerfeld cost him dearly and set him on the path to radicalization. In 1914, he had hoped to be named the professor at Goettingen. He lost that opportunity in a humiliating battle with Sommerfeld, who arranged for a favorite student, Peter Derbye, to be appointed to the post. Gaining nothing for his effort, Stark claimed that the unfortunate outcome was attributable to a "Jewish and pro-Semitic circle and its enterprising business manager [Sommerfeld]." He had to settle for a professorship at the less well-regarded University of Greifswald in 1917.

Following the war, Stark took up conservative politics in earnest. He eventually became the professor of physics in Wuerzburg, where one of Lenard's lifelong adversaries, Wilhelm Conrad Roentgen, had long been the chair. Stark and the University of Wuerzburg were a poor match nearly from the start. Unlike Greifswald, where the faculty was quite conservative, the political atmosphere at the University of Wuerzburg was mostly liberal. Stark's disappointment with the views of his Wuerzburg colleagues and nationally among the members of the German Physical Society led to him organizing the reactionary German Professional Community of University Physicists. In doing so, he unnecessarily alienated any number of natural scientists whose support might have stood him in good stead during his later years of struggle.

Stark might have weathered the philosophical disputes, but the scientific differences between Stark and the Wuerzburg faculty were considerable and, ultimately, unbridgeable. Many of the natural scientists had fully embraced the new theoretical physics. As such, they could be disdainful of the simplistic notions held by classical, experimental physicists. When Stark accepted the thesis of his student Ludwig Glazer on the optical properties of porcelain, his colleagues cried foul on several grounds. Foremost, they questioned whether the topic really represented a sufficient advance to warrant granting an advanced university degree. They charged the topic was too applied, too simplistically practical. They mocked Stark for conferring a "doctorate of porcelain."

They also had qualms about Stark's motivations, charging that it was Glazer's right-wing politics, so akin to Stark's own, that had led to Stark's acceptance of Glazer's work. Lastly, it was discovered that several years earlier, Stark had invested heavily in a porcelain-manufacturing concern. Even though the rules concerning conflicts of interest were lax in those times, this revelation earned him considerable criticism. Something of a hothead, and holding little sway with his faculty, Stark concluded that the University of Wuerzburg was a nest of "Einstein-lovers" and resigned his chair.

Shortly after leaving his position in Wuerzburg in 1923 and entering the commercial sector, Stark published a book that would dog him for its intemperance and help to ensure that, despite applying for six different university appointments over the next decade, he would not receive serious consideration for another academic post until Hitler came to power in 1933. *The Current Crisis in German Physics* heavily criticized theoretical physics and its practitioners. He had earlier reversed his support for quantum theory, and he now attacked it with a vengeance, citing it along with relativity theory as topics that should be banned from the educational curriculum throughout Germany.

Stark also drew unflattering parallels between the theory of relativity and certain social, moral, and political changes occurring at the time, referred to as "relativism." This was a common theme among relativity naysayers. At the core of relativism is the absence of absolutes in morality, acceptable behavior, and philosophy, a fearful thought for many stolid German Protestants.

Stark doubtlessly understood that relativity had nothing to do with relativism, but he exploited the homonymic similarity of the two words as one more reason to be suspicious of Einstein's work. He resurrected Lenard's now familiar complaint that Einstein had unduly promoted the theory of relativity in the "un-German" popular press. While the text fell short of outright anti-Semitic statements, the message came through clearly: the Jews were at the heart of what Stark considered the "crisis."

Because of the stir it caused, many more scientists likely read Max von Laue's review of Stark's book in the journal *Die Nurwissenshaften* than actually read the book itself. Von Laue, a well-respected professor of physics at the University of Berlin, had received the 1914 Nobel Prize for demonstrating that X-rays were diffracted by crystals. Von Laue's assessment of the book dismissed the attacks on his friend Einstein as unworthy of comment. However, he took Stark to task for making unfavorable comments about physics and physicists:

> But Mr. Stark should really have preserved enough respect for his own former activity to not debase it publicly. . . . This severance [his resigning at Wuerzburg] surely did not take place without some conflict. . . . All in all, we would have wished that this book had remained unwrit-

ten, that is, in the interest of science, in general, of German science, in particular, and not least of all in the interest of the author, himself.

During the 1920s and into the next decade, as the frequency and stridency of their attacks intensified, Lenard and Stark recruited junior scientists who were aligned with their philosophy or whom they could bully into joining them in writing articles reflecting their personal point of view. One example is an article by a student of Stark's, Willi Menzel, following the publication of Lenard's *Deutsche Physik*. In the January 29, 1936, edition of *Volkischer Beobachter*, Menzel virtually parroted sections of Lenard's introduction to his book, making assertions identical to Lenard's but framing them as his own. Ambitious and venal, Menzel proved a willing accomplice to Lenard and Stark's attacks:

> In the wake of the revolution in physics came theoreticians like Einstein who then strove to make physics into a purely mathematical system of concepts. They propagated their ideas in the manner characteristic of Jews and forced them upon physicists. They tried to ridicule men who criticized their new type of science with the argument that their intellect just could not aspire to the lofty spheres of the Einsteinian intellect—an intellect which says that Lenard does not consciously seek after the truth.

The recruitment of Lenard's colleagues to his call to arms is most evident in Lenard's 1929 diatribe, *One Hundred Authors against Einstein*, an omnibus of naysayers' views of Einstein's theories. The hundred "authors" of the title were a mixed bag, at best. Many of the contributors had little or no experience with high-energy physics. As noted by reviewer Albert von Braun, the inclusion of many of the authors was absurd:

> Since zero always yields zero when multiplied by any finite number, the compilers might just as well have presented one thousand rather than one hundred of such authors without even the quintessence of their remarks being able to yield any weight other than zero.

Exuding the palpable disdain of a practiced wit, von Braun continued with a withering analogy:

> They should have realized that just as it is true that a majority of votes at a ladies' tea party can scarcely confirm Einstein's theories, in the same way, the accumulation of verdicts by authors who command a little phraseology of Kant's critical philosophy but who have not felt even a whisper of his genius can hardly present a case against relativity theory.

More laconically, Einstein rejoined, "If I were wrong, one would have been enough."

Over more than a decade of harassing Einstein and condemning the Jewish influence in science, Lenard and Stark built a résumé that ingratiated them to the Nazi Party hierarchy. They had stationed themselves where they needed to be to take advantage should Adolf Hitler ever ascend to power. There were long odds against this happening when Lenard and Stark wrote their 1924 honorific, "The Hitler Spirit and Science." Nonetheless, history eventually proved their faith to be well founded.

The Nazi takeover of government provided Lenard and Stark with an unprecedented platform to express their concerns about the undue influence of Jews in Germany's universities. They escalated their vitriolic rants about the threat to German culture by the intrusion of Jewish science. Lenard wrote in the popular right-wing daily *Volkischer Beobachter*:

> It had grown dark in physics. . . . Einstein has provided the most outstanding example of the damaging influence on natural science from the Jewish side. . . . One cannot even spare splendid researchers with solid accomplishments the reproach that they have allowed the relativity Jew to gain a foothold in Germany. . . . Theoreticians active in leading positions should have watched over this development more carefully. Now Hitler is watching over it. The ghost has collapsed; the foreign element is already voluntarily leaving the universities, yes even the country.

Within a week of Hitler declaring himself Fuehrer, Stark wrote Lenard that it was time that they press home their new advantage. They should proceed with their plans to make science more German. Lenard visited Hitler soon after he became Fuehrer. They told him that the German universities had decayed badly. There was a need to develop talented new faculty and expel those who were unworthy. They lobbied for the Reich's adoption of the principles of *Deutsche Physik*, Lenard's pseudo-scientific philosophical construct touting the superiority of the Aryan race and denigrating Jewish scientific thought, which Lenard would publish in four volumes during the following year of 1934.

Hitler welcomed the conversation. He had an interest in science, at least on a philosophical level. He believed that science and religion were locked in an unceasing confrontation. There can be no doubt about which side of the struggle he favored. "If, in the course of a thousand or two thousand years," he asserted in *Mein Kampf*, "Science arrives at the necessity of renewing its points of view, it will not mean that science is a liar. Science cannot lie, for it is always striving, according to the momentary state of knowledge, to deduce what is true. When it makes a mistake, it does so in good faith. It's Christianity that's the liar. It's in perpetual conflict with itself."

Hitler agreed with Lenard's concept of *Deutsche Physik*. Indeed, well before Lenard's vision had fully developed, Hitler had independently written in *Mein Kampf*,

> All human culture, all the results of art, science and technology that we see before us today, are almost exclusively the creative product of the Aryan. This very fact admits of the not unfounded inference that he alone was the founder of all higher humanity, representing the prototype of all that we understand by the word "man."

Hitler took every opportunity to connect his philosophy with the mythological past and fancied himself something of a romantic. In the following passage, he laid it on thickly:

He is the Prometheus of mankind from whose shining brow the divine
spark of genius has sprung at all times, forever kindling anew that fire
of knowledge which illuminated the night of silent mysteries and thus
caused man to climb the path to mastery over the other beings of the
earth. It was he who laid the foundations and erected the walls of every
great structure in human culture.

Lenard and Stark struck a respondent chord in their conversations with
the Fuehrer and his top leadership throughout the 1930s, as the Nazi
hierarchy sought to conduct scientific policy at the behest of racial ideol-
ogy. As late as July 1937, Stark collaborated with Gunter d'Alquen, the
editor of the SS weekly *Das Schwarze Korps*, in writing for that publication an article entitled "White Jews in Science." The article proclaimed
that it was not enough to simply exclude Jews from German cultural life.
Rather, the threat was severe enough that the Reich must extinguish the
Jewish spirit as represented by Albert Einstein.

"There is one sphere, in particular," the authors said, "where we meet
the spirit of the white Jew" (meaning a non-Jew who thought like a Jew
and was supportive of Jewish thinking) "in its most intensive form . . .
namely in science. To purge science from this Jewish spirit is our most
urgent task. For science represents the key position from which intellectual Judaism can always regain a significant influence on all spheres of
national life." They named Planck and Sommerfeld, among others, as
white Jews and concluded, "They must be got rid of as much as the Jews
themselves."

In what must surely rank as one of the most bizarre editorial decisions
ever made by a scientific journal editor, Sir Richard Gregory, then the
editor of *Nature*, one of the world's most respected and most read medical and scientific journals, followed up on Stark's article in *Das Schwarze
Korps* by asking him if he wouldn't care to expand on his views in
Nature's commentary section. Specifically, he asked Stark to write on the
topic of "the Jewish influence on science in Germany or elsewhere."
Stark took him up on it. His article, "The Pragmatic and Dogmatic Spirit
in Physics" asserted that "the manner in which physical research is carried out and described depends on the spirit and character of the men of

science engaged upon it, and this spirit and character differ individually, as do men, nations, and races."

Stark described two "mentalities" in science. The pragmatic mentality began and ended in reality. As representatives of the pragmatic mentality, he named Philipp Lenard and Ernest Rutherford, the New Zealand–born English physicist who detailed the principles of nuclear decay and provided insights into the structure of the atom. He then described the antipodal mentality, which he dubbed "the dogmatic." Here, he named Einstein and Erwin Schroedinger as exemplars.

Stark's choice of Schroedinger is an interesting one. Schroedinger was awarded the 1933 Nobel Prize in physics just after he had left Germany in protest of Hitler's policies in general and the dismissal of physicist Max Born from his university position in particular. The Nazis did not forget this slight. After brief stays at Oxford and Princeton, in 1936, he unwisely accepted an appointment as professor of physics at the University of Graz in Austria. His life was endangered by Hitler's 1938 Anschluss uniting Austria and Germany. Schroedinger managed to escape with his family via Italy and ultimately finished out his career in the newly created Institute for Advanced Studies in Dublin.

In *Nature*, Stark wrote,

> [The dogmatic scientist] starts out from ideas that have arisen primarily in his own brain or from arbitrary relationships among symbols to which a general and so also a physical significance can be ascribed. . . . The pragmatic spirit advances continuously to new discoveries and new knowledge; the dogmatic leads to crippling of experimental research and to a literature which is as effusive as it is unfruitful and tedious, intrinsically akin to the theological dogmatism of the Middle Ages.

Making direct reference to one of Lenard's frequent complaints about Einstein, Stark asserted, "The pragmatic spirit does not conduct propaganda for the results of his research. . . . He finds his satisfaction in obtaining new knowledge." Stark argued that the opposite held true for dogmatic scientists, who, "almost before they have published, a flood of propaganda is started."

Stark had taken it upon himself to save German culture from Einstein and his dogmatic imitators. "I also have directed my efforts against the damaging influence of Jews in German science, because I regard them as the chief exponents and propagandists of the dogmatic spirit." One might imagine that these lines would have set off *Nature*'s publication of a firestorm of correspondence from those who wished to take issue with such an extreme view, including the many Jewish scientists who had by then immigrated to the United States, Great Britain, and elsewhere in Europe. However, that was not the case. *Nature* published only a single letter, and that one appeared six months after the appearance of Stark's article.

Given Hitler's mandate, Lenard and Stark continued the drumbeat against Einstein and, by proxy, all Jewish scientists. Despite his having emigrated weeks before the passage of the Enabling Law, Einstein remained the principal target of Lenard's and Stark's attacks as the living embodiment of Jewish scientific depravity. He would remain so until their influence declined nearly two decades after Einstein and Lenard first confronted each other at Bad Nauheim.

Lenard's resentment of Einstein's success and his rabid anti-Semitism underlay his purge of Jewish academics that began soon after Einstein fled to America. His assertion of Aryan scientific supremacy, couched in the principles of *Deutsche Physik*, gained currency among the Nazi leadership. The resultant policies proved popular among many of Germany's natural scientists, who, in the short term, prospered in the absence of competition with the Jewish scientists they replaced. In the bizarre world of Aryan science, lesser talents could succeed without having to confront the mathematical intricacies of theoretical physics or the probing questions of talented Jewish theorists.

Lenard, however, viewed the transition from Jewish to Aryan scientists from a very different perspective. Despite the fact that he was disdainful of the talents of most Aryan physicists to the point of being unable to recommend them for the numerous vacant university positions, the triumph of the Aryan physicist was inevitable. The Jewish mind suffered an important inherent deficiency. In 1940, he wrote in the margins of his 1922 edition of *Ether and Urether*,

> How artificial as scientists those physicists must indeed be who still today hold a "theory" with such sappy jests about space and time to be important. Sappy, I say, because it in the essence underlies the Jewish inability with space and time. . . . Just as the cubists had an inability to paint decently, so here lies together the audacity and the inability they want to impose on others.

Upon Einstein's departure, Lenard wrote a letter to Reichsminister for Public Enlightenment and Propaganda Joseph Goebbels, calling for the enforced abolition of all relics of Einstein and his theory of relativity, as well as the dismissal of any supporter of Einstein from his academic post—Jew or non-Jew. To do otherwise, he argued, would be politically dangerous.

Lenard and Stark would get their way. They would live to see German science performed as they had hoped, by Aryan Germans, at least for a while.

11

DEUTSCHE PHYSIK

"'German Physics?' You will ask. I could also have said Aryan physics or physics of the Nordic type of peoples, physics of the probers of reality, of truth seekers, the physics of those who have founded scientific research," wrote Philipp Lenard at the outset of his four-volume master work, *Deutsche Physik*.

To those unfamiliar with the history of science, Lenard's opening thrust must seem an odd assertion. As opposed to pursuits like literature, philosophy, and history, where cultural imprints are inevitable, shouldn't science be blind to the national origins of the research that defines its progress? How could it be otherwise? Some new bit of knowledge discovered in Germany is published in an English language journal and read in Korea, where researchers use the new information to redesign what had been to that point futile investigations. The German discovery makes all the difference in the Korean experiments, and mans' understanding of his universe advances another small step forward.

Predicting this response, Lenard assumed responsibility for both sides of the debate:

> "Science is international, and it will always remain so," you will want
> to protest. But this is inevitably based on a fallacy. In reality, as with
> everything that man creates, science is determined by race or by blood.
> It can seem to be international when universally valid scientific results
> are wrongly traced to a common origin or when it is not acknowledged

that science supplied by peoples of different countries is identical or similar to German science, and that science could only have been produced because and to the extent that other peoples are or were likewise of a predominantly Nordic racial mix. Nations of different racial mixes practice science differently.

The roots of *Deutsche Physik* can be traced to a particularly shocking episode that occurred during World War I. The ensuing disagreement as to whom was at fault advanced nationalistic fervor among Europe's leading scientists and set the foundations for the internecine scientific struggles that occurred in the postwar period. The 1839 Treaty of London guaranteed Belgium neutral status in continental wars. However, Germany's military brain trust recognized that, by going through Belgium, it might outflank the French army, which was concentrated in eastern France. Calling the treaty "a scrap of paper," German Chancellor Theobold von Beckmann Hollweg sent his armies into Belgium. What followed has become known as the "rape of Belgium." One and a half million Belgians fled from the invading German army. Six thousand Belgian civilians died. The onslaught destroyed twenty-five thousand buildings.

The Germans had overrun Leuven in Belgium but were having trouble controlling an unruly populace. Belgian guerrilla fighters attacked without warning, exacted their damage, and disappeared into the narrow alleyways of the ancient city. Casualties mounted among the German troops at an alarming rate. The German army adopted a harsh policy of reprisals toward Belgian civilians that, on the night of August 25, 1914, culminated in the commission of wholesale atrocities. The invaders evicted as many as ten thousand Belgians from their homes, looted the Leuven food supplies, and set fire to two thousand houses. They also set fire to the library of the Katholieke Universiteit Leuven, the repository of hundreds of thousands of rare books and irreplaceable medieval manuscripts.

The torching of Leuven set off a worldwide outcry. In the wake of England having declared war on Germany just three weeks earlier, a number of well-known British academics published a brief note in the

Times of London protesting the destruction. Among the scientists signing the letter were William Crookes, who had briefly hosted Lenard in his laboratory during Lenard's years of peripatetic training, and J. J. Thompson, a Nobel laureate for his work on elucidating the electron.

The German backlash was immediate and vigorous. England was responsible for the war. The English were trying to shift the blame for the war onto the shoulders of their most effective economic competitor. Writers Ludwig Fulda, Hermann Sudermann, and Georg Reicke drafted the "Manifesto of the Ninety-three German Intellectuals." The Manifesto, which received wide publication in newspapers throughout Europe, denied that the destruction of the Leuven library had been purposeful. Indeed, it was inconceivable that German soldiers could be responsible for wartime atrocities:

> As representatives of German Science and Art, we hereby protest to the civilized world against the lies and calumnies with which our enemies are endeavoring to stain the honor of Germany in her hard struggle for existence—in a struggle that has been forced on her. . . . As heralds of truth we raise our voices against these.

Among the denials that followed were that Germany did not cause the current conflict, had not injured or killed a single Belgian citizen "without the bitterest defense having made it necessary," and had not "without aching hearts" set fire to a portion of the city. The document concludes,

> We cannot wrest the poisonous weapon—the lie—out of the hands of our enemies. All we can do is to proclaim to the world that our enemies are giving false witness against us. Have faith in us! Believe that we shall carry on this war to the end as a civilized nation to whom the legacy of a Goethe, a Beethoven, and a Kant is just as sacred as its own hearth and home.

Among those signing the Manifesto were the flower of German physics, including Nobel Prize recipients Wilhelm Wien, Max Planck, Wilhelm Conrad Roentgen, and Philipp Lenard. The Manifesto reflected a compromise among widely divergent viewpoints. There were those who feared that a too strongly worded document would incite a permanent backlash that would hinder relationships between scientists of different nationalities beyond the end of the war. In this camp was Max Planck. He was away from Berlin at the time but decided to lend his name to the Manifesto based on what Wien had told him; he asked his children to sign in his absence. Several years later, he regretted this decision and publicly reneged on his signature. A 1921 *New York Times* survey revealed that a number of other signatories felt the same way. Sixty of seventy-six intellectuals who survived the war either regretted their participation or claimed they had not so much as seen what they had signed.

Others felt that the document fell short of the necessary measures. Wien advocated a boycott of English journals and establishing rules prohibiting the use of English words in German scientific papers. Lenard, who donated the money he'd received with the Royal Society's Rumford Medal to the families of fallen soldiers, favored a more strongly worded document. Lenard had by this time severed old ties with J. J. Thompson, believing that the Cambridge don had given him insufficient credit for his work on the electron. Lenard's 1914 booklet, "England and Germany in the Time of the Great War," attacked German scientists for too often crediting English investigators for discoveries made in Germany.

Equating the veracity of Englishmen with that of Jews, Lenard warned that should the enemy perceive any sign of weakness,

> The English gentlemen will smile internally with pleasure over our timidity when they see the Proclamation. Externally, they will naturally pull some sort of swindle. Should something really forcefully be done, I will be happy to participate. I think these liars are not worth the waste of time, except with cannons.

The actions of the "ninety-three" were amplified when, on October 16, 1914, four thousand university teachers, nearly all of the faculty members of the fifty-three German universities, signed "The Declaration of University Teachers of the German Empire." The intent of the Declaration was to remove any doubt in the minds of Germany's enemies: German academics stood foursquare with their national army; there was no philosophical division between the thinking of German professors and that of the German military.

Perhaps because of his Swiss citizenship, or possibly because his contrary views were well known, Einstein was not asked to sign either the "Manifesto" or the "Declaration." He was the antithesis of a patriotic nationalist, an internationalist who believed that overweening nationalism—especially as practiced in his native Germany—led to unchecked militarism. An armed German military bolstered by universal military conscription was a threat to European stability.

Shocked by the destruction of the Leuven library, angry about the anti-British sentiments expressed by some of the signers, and outraged by the chauvinistic attitudes of many of his colleagues, Einstein joined with a physician friend, Georg Friedrich Nicolai, to write a countermanifesto, "An Appeal to the Europeans." The purpose of the "Appeal" was to advocate for peace in Europe and the honoring of existing borders among countries; it drew only four signatures. The document was never published in Germany. Its publication outside of Germany was delayed until 1917, and it quickly disappeared from public consciousness.

The Leuven matter and the prolonged deprivations of the Great War polarized Germany's scientists into opposing camps. As Einstein became more active as an internationalist and pacifist, Lenard grew more reactionary. Amid Germany's postwar economic deterioration and the consequent decline in his own finances, Lenard embraced the popular notion that it was the socialists and Jews who were pulling the strings of government and laying waste to the German economy. In the aftermath of World War I and over the next fifteen years, Lenard developed his beliefs about the distinctions between the Aryan scientific mind and that of the alien "other."

The 1934 publication of the first volume of *Deutsche Physik* must have been a tremendous catharsis for the seventy-two-year-old scientist. Although Lenard's expressed purpose in writing *Deutsche Physik* was to summarize a lifetime of lectures on experimental physics—which by all accounts were virtuoso performances—he wrote the foreword to the first volume as a crystallization of his philosophy of Aryan scientific supremacy. Headed by an unattributed epigram—"The foreword stems from to-day's conflict / The work seeks value infinite"—the author, more explicitly than ever before, communicated his alarm about the threat the "Jewish spirit" posed to the purity of the natural sciences and, hence, all of German culture. *Deutsche Physik* was based on several principles that Lenard took to be inviolable.

First, all worthy scientific discoveries were attributable to Aryans. Non-Aryan science might initially be based on the successes of Aryans, but over time, each non-Aryan culture or ethnicity developed distinctive hallmarks of inferiority:

> [No] people ever embarked on scientific research without basing themselves on the fertile ground of already existing Aryan achievements. . . . The racial characteristics of these foreign forms only become recognizable after they have developed over a longer period. Based on the available literature, one could, perhaps, already talk about Japanese physics. Arabian physics existed in the past. Nothing has yet emerged about Negro physics. Jewish physics has developed and become prevalent, which has only rarely been recognized until now.

Second, meaningful science was based on experimentation. Aryan research began and ended with observation and measurement. Simplicity, grounded in nature, was a hallmark of *Deutsche Physik*. In contrast, scientific theories based on mathematical representations were antithetical to Aryan science in that they failed Lenard's test of "common sense." They resided only in the abstract. They contributed nothing new. They baffled rather than illuminated.

> All the well-verified knowledge of inorganic nature can be found here [in *Deutsche Physik*] in a uniform and totally coherent text. . . . The unspoiled German national spirit [Volksgeist] seeks depth; it seeks theoretical foundations consistent with nature and irrefutable knowledge of the cosmos. . . . Thinking along with nature—following its processes systematically—is very seldom done correctly. Usually you are confronted with formulae instead. It is peculiar to see physics texts

filled with mathematical derivations that offer absolutely nothing about the origin, value, and significance of the topic.

A third tenet was that it was the encroachment of Jews, who secretly and maliciously had hidden their physics, which now posed a threat to German culture. "At the end of the Great War," Lenard wrote, "when Jews in Germany began to dominate and set the tone, the full force of its [Jewish physics] characteristics suddenly burst forth like a flood. It then promptly found avid supporters even among many authors of non-Jewish or not really pure Jewish blood."

In the world of *Deutsche Physik*, Aryan scientists' sole motivation for their research was the elucidation of truth. Others, particularly Jews, had more nefarious motives and were not above lying and self-promotion:

> The characteristic haste of the Jewish mentality to come up with un-
> tested ideas was actually contagious; though it provides personal ad-
> vantages (Jewish applause, primarily), it has a negative effect on the
> whole. In Jewish physics, every assumption that proves not to be com-
> pletely false is celebrated as a milestone.

Explaining how the Jews cunningly gained ascendency in physics, Lenard revived past complaints about Einstein, who, despite his having immigrated to the United States, was still "the unquestionably full-blooded Jew." He wrote,

> [The Jew's science] is only an illusion and a degenerate manifestation
> of fundamental Aryan science [that treats truth and lies as] equivalent
> to any one of the many different theoretical options available. . . . This
> fact was concealed through computational tricks. . . . The characteristic
> audacity of the uninhibited Jew, together with the deft collaboration of
> his fellow Jews, [which] enabled the construction of Jewish physics.

Finally, Lenard concluded that, even allowing for the sorry state of the natural sciences, Aryan science would inevitably prevail:

> But a people that has produced the likes of [among others] Copernicus,
> Kepler . . . Leibnitz, Mendel, and [one of his own mentors] Bunsen

will know how to find itself again, just as it has found a Fuehrer of its own blood in politics as heir to Frederick the Great and Bismarck, who saved it from the chaos of Marxism, which is equally alien, racially.

Deutsche Physik was a crystallization of Lenard's thoughts and experiences during two decades of rising nationalism among German scientists during and following World War I. He had, for more than a decade, included bits and pieces of similar content in his speeches and writings of what he now comprehensively published in *Deutsche Physik*. Despite having done so, he had managed to convince only a handful of acolytes, while many Aryans had flocked to the theoretical physics of Einstein.

Now, however, *Deutsche Physik* was an idea whose time had come. The publication of the foreword to *Deutsche Physik* coincided nearly perfectly with Hitler becoming Fuehrer, and its content was convergent with the beliefs of Germany's new leadership. Suddenly, there were receptive ears at the highest level of government. Born out of envy, bitterness, and prejudice, *Deutsche Physik* appeared at exactly the right time to provide the philosophical underpinnings for the self-destructive scientific policies of the Third Reich.

Immediately upon Hitler's appointment as Chancellor, Lenard and Stark sought to impress their views upon the Nazi hierarchy. The biggest problem in their minds was that the Jews had gained ascendancy in the German universities and, for years, had been fostering the careers of their own kind. There was a paucity of capable, well-trained Aryans who could reasonably fill the openings that would develop under *Deutsche Physik*. Even so, Lenard would do his best to ensure the start of what would become a renewal of Aryan leadership in German universities.

At seventy-one, Lenard was not particularly interested in new titles or responsibilities. His goal was to see completed what he had imagined— the complete vanquishing of Einstein and the extinction of his work, followed by a renewal of German academe along the lines of *Deutsche Physik*. This was not the case for his younger protégé, Johannes Stark. Stark sought more concrete authority from a personal acquaintance, Minister of the Interior Wilhelm Frick. His goal was to be appointed to several high positions where he could control virtually all appointments to university professorships and government research funding throughout Germany.

As his opening gambit, Stark petitioned Frick to appoint him president of Germany's Reich Physical and Technical Institute, a title he had long coveted. However, his troubles in Wuerzburg and the long memory of his ill-advised 1922 publication of *The Current Crisis in German Physics* had caused him to be passed over for the position on two occasions during the preceding decade. The institute was a central resource for all of German science, doling out equipment, personnel, and money for research throughout the German university system. Despite the unanimous opposition of every scientist consulted, Minister Frick appointed Stark as president in May 1933.

Lenard celebrated Stark's appointment by writing an opinion article for the politically sympathetic newspaper *Voelkischer Beobachter* entitled, "A Big Day for Science: Johannes Stark Appointed President of the Reich Physical and Technical Institute." Noting that the appointment represented a political reversal from the norm during the Weimar Republic, he wrote that Stark becoming president

> signifies a renunciation of the apparently already inescapable predominance of what briefly might be called Einsteinian thinking in physics, and it is a move towards reaffirming the scientist's old prerogatives: to think independently, guided only by nature. . . . Stark, one of the remaining untouched examples of this thinking is himself at the top in such an important post. . . . Not only science may rejoice in this way. Technology also is done a great service in now having Stark at the head of the Reich Physical and Technical Institute. For he is not only an outstanding scholar and accomplished researcher but also, at the same time, a practitioner. . . . In all likelihood, never before has such a suitable choice been made for president.

The institute's interim administration had presaged the new president's expected actions by firing all Jewish employees, which freed Stark to take immediate steps toward further Aryanization of its faculty. He reduced the institute's investment in theoretical physics, instituted a rigid hierarchical organizational structure with himself as the chief of the natural sciences, and fired the Jewish members of the institute's advisory committee. The subsequent dissolution of the committee gave Stark absolute authority. He developed plans for a massive expansion to further accrue power for his domain.

By the time the German Physical Society met in Wuerzburg in September 1933, Lenard and Stark had leveraged their relationships with the National Socialists so they could effectively control access to all university appointments, as well as the share of governmental research funding distributed through Stark's institute. A presentation by Stark at the meeting introduced his idea for organizing research in the natural sciences. Noting that his Reich Physical and Technical Institute already was charged with communicating with and servicing the needs of all of the other physics departments in Germany, he proposed that—for the good of the country—the institute extend its responsibilities:

> It is from this central, comprehensive, and leading position that its responsibility arises to organize physical research for the benefit of both science and industry. Some of my listeners may well immediately object to the term "organization of scientific research." The question might be raised: Can scientific research be organized at all? Surely, scientific progress is always the independent achievement of individuals. . . . These statements are certainly correct. But they misinterpret the purpose of scientific organization.

Stark wished to reorganize science in the Reich by adopting the "Fuehrer principle," Already implemented in a number of spheres, the Fuehrer principle emulated the steeply vertical hierarchy of the highest level of the German government. Stark proposed that the Reich Physical and Technical Institute be greatly expanded to centralize and manage resources across the expanse of Germany. Among a long list of responsibilities he felt the institute should assume were to unite the various institutes and academic departments of physics throughout Germany; serve as the necessary mediator between them and as the intended source of ideas or support; greatly increase its size and scope, with a goal of quadrupling its capacity in order to "exercise its duty to science and the economy"; serve as a central resource for equipment and manpower for investigations that were beyond the capabilities of individual departments; and "act as an agent between physical research and industry."

He saved the best for nearly the end. Much to the chagrin of his audience, in the last few minutes of his address to Germany's physicists, Stark suggested the following:

> Furthermore, the Reich Physical and Technical Institute will be involved in the monitoring of physical literature, since changes must be made to protect German physics within Germany, as well as to maintain its influence abroad.

After once more invoking the beneficence of Minister Frick and his hope for the support of Fuehrer Hitler, he asked for his audience's understanding and assistance:

> But I also need your support, gentlemen. You, my colleagues also can assist directly or indirectly in the organization [and funding decisions] of the German Research Foundation and in the reorganization of publication in physics. I ask for your cooperation in the projected organization of physical research for the benefit and honor of the German people.

Somewhat obtusely, Stark was proposing a central clearinghouse for all research manuscripts seeking publication in German journals. This was very much along the lines of what Goebbels had established for the lay press, where the Fuehrer principle was firmly entrenched. In the end, Stark was not so much asking for his audience's assent as informing them of his plans. He quoted a verse of Goethe's "Erlkoenig": ". . . and if you are not willing, I will use force." To further clarify his intent, he stated, "The Fuehrer now takes over the responsibility for the Fatherland, I will now take over the responsibility for physics."

Although Stark assured those attending that the purpose of his plan was to ensure freedom of research and publication, his speech provoked considerable unease, especially on the part of the theoretical physicists. Max von Laue challenged Stark, comparing his crusade against Einstein and relativity to the Catholic Church's efforts to silence Galileo and to ban Copernicus' view that the earth revolved around the sun. Regardless of *Deutsche Physik*, and as hard as Stark might try to suppress them, Einstein's theories were still correct. An angered Lenard attributed the supportive applause for von Laue to "Jews and their fellow travelers present."

While the disrespect of his peers doubtlessly offended him, Stark persisted in his ambitions. He had further developed his relationships with individuals at the top levels of government. Like Lenard, he had direct access to Hitler. Hitler gave his preliminary approval to Stark's grandiose plans for expanding the Reich Institute. However, academic infighting and a lack of available moneys eventually proved to be insuperable barriers, and Stark's plans never were actualized.

In the spring of 1934, Stark realized the second of his major goals. He was appointed chair of the German Research Foundation, which had succeeded the Emergency Foundation as the principal national funding agency for research grants in the natural sciences. Hitler himself gave the order for the dismissal of Friedrich Schmidt-Ott from the post, "because the Fuehrer wishes it," and Schmidt-Ott's replacement by Stark.

Lenard rejoiced at the news. For all practical purposes, Stark now controlled both faculty hiring and access to the funds necessary for German faculty to conduct research. Lenard had Hitler's ear and was to become the "kingmaker," the one to decide which professors were suitable for employment and where they should be assigned. Together, he and Stark could continue to develop the natural sciences in German universities according to the principles of *Deutsche Physik*.

Stark used his new power without restraint. As his first action, Stark ceased research funding for all theoretical work and even restricted what experimental work got funded to "Aryan" topics. He frequently reversed committee recommendations to fund a project with a terse "President Stark requests rejection," with no further explanation.

For the next several years, as *Deutsche Physik* held sway, Lenard and Stark were riding high. In December 1935, when the two colleagues were enjoying their greatest influence, Stark was offered the chance to speak about how far the tenets of *Deutsche Physik* had taken Germany. On the occasion of the University of Heidelberg renaming its Institute of Physics the Philipp Lenard Institute, Stark revived the face of villainy that had weathered so many of his speeches to personalize his fears for German society. Stark took the opportunity to revile Albert Einstein and, by proxy, Jewish science:

> A large group of people, primarily in physics, believe that to be able to arrive at results, or at least to come up with impressive articles . . . they must produce a mathematically lavishly dressed theory. . . . This type of approach is consistent with the Jewish peculiarity of making their own opinion, their own desires and advantage into the measure of all things and thus of scientific knowledge, as well.

Stark's remarks to this point were covering familiar ground. Well into his address, Stark decided to take a chance by naming possible new targets for his future attentions:

> Jewish physics . . . has been practiced and propagated by Jews, as well as their non-Jewish students and emulators, which logically have also found its high priest in a Jew, Einstein. Jewish propaganda has tried to portray him as the greatest scientist of all time. However, Einstein's relativity theories were basically nothing more than an accumulation of artificial formulas based on arbitrary definitions. . . The sensation and propaganda of the Einsteinian relativity theory was followed by Heisenberg's matrix theory and Schroedinger's so-called wave mechanics, one as impenetrable and formalistic as the next . . . however, it has contributed no important new knowledge. This could not have been otherwise, since its point of departure, formalistic human opinion, was false.

Except for the younger timbre to his voice, an observer listening with eyes closed would be forgiven for mistaking Stark for Lenard. The day fairly bristled with the rhetoric of *Deutsche Physik*. There was a self-congratulatory air that must have given Stark a special level of confidence. He lauded Lenard for publicly facing down Einstein in the *Ein-*

steindebatte at Bad Nauheim and spoke of Einstein's flight from his homeland. He spoke out against several respected scientists whom he called Einstein's "German friends and supporters" and won encouraging cheers from his sympathetic audience by accusing them of continuing to act "in his spirit."

Stark pointed out that Einstein's main supporter, Planck, was still at the head of the Kaiser Wilhelm Society; his expounder and friend, Max von Laue, was still permitted to act as referee in physics at the Berlin Academy of Sciences; and the theoretical formalist, Heisenberg, whom he depicted as the essence of Einstein's spirit, was supposed to be honored with a professorship. In view of these regrettable circumstances, which contradicted the National Socialist spirit, Lenard's struggle against Einsteinianism should have been a warning. The responsible official advisors at the Culture Ministry had erred. It would have been much better if they had consulted with Philipp Lenard before filling professorial chairs in physics, including those in theoretical physics.

By this time, Planck and von Laue were so well established as to be untouchable, but Heisenberg was not. In designating Heisenberg the essence of Einstein's spirit, and later calling him a "white Jew," Stark was telegraphing a battle that had already begun. In choosing Heisenberg as his foe, Stark unknowingly had imperiled both his own standing among the National Socialists and the continued influence of *Deutsche Physik*.

12

ACADEMIC IMPURITIES

At 10:45 on the morning of May 16, 1933, Max Planck's driver helped the dean of German physicists from the backseat of his car. Planck stepped onto the curb of Berlin's Wilhelmstrasse, running alongside the Chancellery. Despite a cold, gusting wind tickling his memory of what had been a harsh winter, Planck stood motionless for a brief moment, surveying his surroundings. The Chancellery was an impressive Rococo palace that had served as the seat of German government since 1875. Planck once thought its graceful symmetry a harmonious example of Prussian architecture. That was no longer the case, not since the Weimar government had erected the crass, modern south wing in 1930. It was a stain that was impossible to ignore. For better or worse, change was inevitable.

As president of the Kaiser Wilhelm Society, Germany's most prestigious scientific organization, Planck had sought the opportunity to speak with Adolf Hitler, the newly appointed Chancellor, "on the current situation and future plans of the Society." He had made certain to arrive at the Chancellor's offices a few minutes early so he could settle his nerves and think about several issues that had arisen since Hitler had taken office. Chief among his concerns was a new law that mandated the dismissal of "non-Aryan civil servants." The word "non-Aryan" was a euphemism for "Jewish." Since all faculty and staff of German universities were classified as "civil servants," the law threatened the continued employment of all Jewish professors. Indiscriminate enforcement of the new law would result in the dismissal of many of Germany's elite physicists, chemists, and mathematicians and irreparably hinder the progress of German science for years to come. This would be Planck's only chance to reason with Hitler. He would need to keep his wits about him if he were to have any chance of getting through to him.

As a secretary ushered him into Hitler's office, Planck considered how he might most effectively address his concerns in a way that Hitler would understand. He decided to use as an example his Jewish colleague, Fritz Haber. The Nobel laureate had recently resigned his university position in protest of the new law. Haber was a national hero for his invention of processes for producing poisonous gases during the Great War, without which Germany would have lost from the start. Planck broached the subject delicately, but Hitler was immediately on the alert. "I have nothing against Jews as such," Hitler said, "But Jews are all communists, and it is the latter who are my enemies; it is against them that my fight is directed."

"There are different types of Jews," Planck said, "Both worthy and worthless ones to humanity, with old families of the highest German culture among the former." He suggested that a distinction should be made between the various sorts.

"That's not right. A Jew is a Jew," Hitler objected. "All Jews stick together like burrs. When there is one Jew, all kinds of other Jews gather right away. It should have been the duty of the Jews themselves to draw a dividing line between the various types. They did not do this, and that is why I must act against all Jews equally."

Planck said, "Forcing worthy Jews to emigrate would be equivalent to mutilating ourselves outright, because we direly need their scientific work, and their efforts would otherwise accrue primarily to the benefit of foreign countries,"

The Chancellor ignored the comment. After an uncomfortable minute, Hitler said, "People say I suffer occasionally from nervous disability. This is slander. I have nerves of steel." As if to prove how sturdy he was, he began to bang his fist on his knee. He spoke extremely fast, beating himself into a great fury. Planck was left with no other choice than to remain silent and to take his leave.

Enacted a month earlier, on April 7, 1933, the Law for the Restoration of the Professional Civil Service had been the brainchild of the Reichsminister of the Interior, Wilhelm Frick. He was the same man to whom Johannes Stark had turned for his appointment to the presidency of the Reich Physical and Technical Institute. The law called for mass dismissals from the civil service of several classes of individuals, without either benefits or pensions. Chief among those scheduled for dismissal were "civil servants who were not of Aryan descent" unless they had already been employed by the civil service prior to August 1, 1914, or "who had fought in the World War at the front for the German Reich or its allies, or whose fathers or sons had been casualties in the World War." Also named were "Civil servants who, based upon their previous political activities, cannot guarantee that they have always unreservedly supported the national state." Finally, the law provided for transfers of individuals to lesser posts—at lower pay—at the discretion of the Reich. These dismissals and transfers were to be carried out no later than September 30, 1933, just months after the law went into effect.

There would be no mistaking the intent of the legislation. A series of "ordinances," representing definitions or amplifications of the law, were issued over the next several months. The first ordinance was issued on April 11, 1933. Its goals were to clarify that "All civil servants who belonged to the communist party or to communist support organizations or substitute organizations are unqualified [for civil service]. They are therefore to be dismissed." The law also grew more precise with regard to defining the term "non-Aryan" as "anyone descended from non-Aryan, and in particular Jewish, parents or grandparents, is considered non-Aryan. It is sufficient [to disqualify a person for service] that one parent or one grandparent be non-Aryan. This is to be assumed especially when one parent or one grandparent has practiced the Jewish Faith."

All officials were to prove their ancestry by presenting certified documents like a birth certificate, the marriage certificate of their parents, or military papers. Finally, if there were some question concerning a civil servant's ancestry, an opinion had to be requested of a "specialist on race research."

The 1933 civil service law was the initial thrust of a comprehensive, long-term Nazi plan to restrict Jews from participation in public life, particularly in highly visible fields like academics, medicine, and law. The 1935 Nuremberg Laws further defined who was considered a Jew, prohibited sexual relations between Aryans and Jews, set quotas for Jewish students' enrollment in universities, and prohibited the granting of doctoral degrees to Jewish students unless they had already completed writing their thesis. Laws passed in 1938 and 1939 completed the isolation of German Jews by forbidding most professional and financial interactions between Jews and non-Jews. For example, Jewish physicians could no longer treat Aryan patients. Loopholes were abolished that had allowed small numbers of Jewish professors to continue in their university positions for past meritorious service during the Great War.

One of the immediate casualties of the new law was Planck's friend Fritz Haber, though his dismissal was self-inflicted. The sixty-five-year-old, 1918 Nobel laureate had revolutionized the production of fertilizer with his reaction of nitrogen and air to produce ammonia. In addition, he had been of great service to the Fatherland, though less so to humanity, with his invention of chlorine and other weaponizable gases, which Germany had used to great effect in World War I.

Haber noted in his April 30, 1933, letter of resignation addressed to the head of the Ministry of Culture, Bernhard Rust, that by dint of his employment as a professor at Berlin University having begun in 1898, he was entitled to remain in office despite having Jewish parents and grandparents. "But I do not wish to make use of this privilege for longer than is necessary to properly dispose of the academic and administrative functions vested in me through my offices," he wrote.

Haber further explained,

> My decision to request my discharge stems from the contrast between the tradition to which I have adhered up to now concerning scientific research and the changed attitudes which you, Mister Minister, and your Ministry represent as the vanguards of the great modern national

> movement. My tradition demands that in my choice of colleagues I take into account the professional and personal attributes of applicants to an academic position without inquiring after their racial characteristics.

Haber closed by reminding the minister of his contributions to Germany. Speaking of himself in the third person, he wrote, "You will understand that the pride with which he has served his German native country throughout his life now compels him to make this request for retirement."

The remainder of Fritz Haber's story is short and sad. Soon after he resigned his faculty position, Haber moved to a temporary lectureship in Cambridge, at least in part to escape the backlash over his resignation among his German colleagues. Soon after his arrival in England, Zionist Chaim Weizmann recruited Haber to the faculty of a new science and technology campus being built south of Tel Aviv, in Israel, that eventually would bear Weizmann's name. Haber had been in ill health and died of heart failure en route to his new home.

Many of Fritz Haber's extended family members would die in German concentration camps. However, his son by his first wife Clara managed to immigrate to the United States. In 1946, Hermann Haber committed suicide over the shame of his father having invented an early version of Zyclon B, the gas the Nazis had used to murder millions of Jews during the Holocaust. His death reprised his mother's, who thirty-one years earlier had shot herself to death after the first combat deployment of Haber's chlorine gas, near Ypern, during the Great War.

In writing his obituary of Haber, Max von Laue drew a parallel between the last years of his friend's complex life and those of Themistocles, who "went down in history not as the pariah at the Court of the Persian king but as the victor of Salamis . . . [Haber] will be remembered as the man who had made bread out of thin air and who triumphed in the service of his country and of the whole of humanity."

Another voluntary resignation drew even greater attention. The April 19, 1933, edition of the *Goettinger Tageblatt* carried the story of Professor James Franck's resignation from Goettingen University. Franck had shared the 1925 Nobel Prize in physics with Gustav Hertz for his work on the interactions of atomic particles. Having once proclaimed that his god was science and nature his religion, Franck saw himself not as a Jew, but as an assimilated German citizen. Nonetheless, under Nazi law he was Jewish. Since he was a World War I veteran who had been decorated with the Iron Cross, First Class, and seriously injured in a gas attack, he was exempt from prosecution under the civil service law.

A number of friends advised Franck to continue in his professorship, arguing that the current situation was only temporary and that it would resolve itself. As one colleague said to him, "Nothing is eaten as hot as it is cooked." Regardless, Franck was determined to resign in protest. He met with several friends to draft his letter of resignation and write a press release the evening before the newspapers broke the story:

> I have requested of my superior that I be released from my office. I will try to continue to work in science in Germany. We Germans of Jewish descent are being treated as foreigners and enemies of the Fatherland. It is expected that our children grow up knowing that they are not permitted ever to prove themselves worthy Germans. Whoever has been in the war is permitted to continue to serve the state. I decline to take advantage of this privilege, even though I understand the position of those who today see it as their duty to stay resolutely at their posts.

The reaction to Franck's resignation was vigorous and immediate. Forty-two of Goettingen's faculty denounced Franck's public withdrawal. Specifically citing Franck's passage about Jews being treated as foreigners and enemies of the Fatherland, their statement read,

> [Franck's resignation] could seriously impede the domestic and foreign political activities of our government of the national renewal. We are in agreement that the form of the above tender of resignation is tantamount to an act of sabotage; and we therefore hope that the Government will carry out the necessary purging measures expeditiously.

The professors responsible for the document went on to explain that "due to the holidays, it was not possible to obtain the signatures of all the professors, but it can be relatively assumed that they approve of the above declaration." The signatories further commented that Franck's resignation had "even irritated his fellow Jews at the *Berliner Tageblatt*, which immediately recognized that Professor Franck had made a fatal step that the Government cannot overlook idly."

Perhaps surprisingly, the *Goettinger Tageblatt* sided with Franck, concluding its coverage as follows: "The decision of Professor Franck is to be rated largely, yes even solely, as a moral one. We hope and wish that this step, by which Franck destroys his life's work and his life's content, will have the effect that other scientists who would be forced to resign by the current regulations are kept for our scientific life."

Franck received numerous private letters of support, but there was no open display of public protest. When fellow physicist Otto Hahn suggested to Planck that the two of them organize a demonstration of solidarity on Franck's behalf, Planck saw only futility: "If you bring together thirty such men today, then tomorrow one hundred-fifty will come to denounce them, because they want to take their places."

Within days, the university dismissed six other Jewish faculty members. It was only the beginning of the initial purge. Despite Franck's desire to continue working in Germany, even if it meant working in industry, no company stepped forward to hire him. Things quickly degenerated for Franck and his family. They faced increasing harassment by brown shirts and neighbors to the point of fearing for their safety. In November 1933, James Franck moved with his wife and daughters to become a professor of physical chemistry at Johns Hopkins University in Baltimore, Maryland. In 1938, Franck moved his family to Chicago, where he could more actively participate in the Manhattan Project. While contributing to the scientific underpinnings of bomb development, he simultaneously chaired the Committee on Political and Social Problems related to the atomic bomb. The committee generated what became known as the Franck Report, recommending that the United States abstain from dropping the atomic bomb on Japanese cities. Franck personally handed the committee's report to Arthur Compton, an assistant to the U.S. Secretary of War Henry Stimson, on June 11, 1945. It is uncertain whether Stimson ever reviewed the report or whether it even was considered in arriving at the decision to drop atomic bombs, without warning, on Japanese population centers.

Franck was appalled by the government's disregard of his committee's report and at the resultant destruction of human life. He spent much of the remainder of his long life arguing for restraint in punishing the vanquished enemy. "The feeling of revenge is, of course, strong in Jewish circles," Franck wrote to his friend, Albert Einstein, after the war. "If that goes on, the Nazis will have won in their battle for demoralization of the whole world. . . . I will have no part in the punishment and gradual elimination of the innocent."

Despite his reputation for pacifism, Einstein would have none of this. Einstein responded, "The Germans slaughtered millions of civilian's according to a carefully conceived plan. . . . They would do it again if they could. The few white ravens among them changes absolutely nothing. . . . Dear Franck! Keep your hands off this foul affair!"

As the resignations of Haber and Franck and the mounting dismissals of Jewish professors began to attract worldwide attention, Johannes Stark, by this time ensconced in the presidency of the Reich Physical and Technical Institute, went on the offensive. It infuriated him that although Jews accounted for less than 1 percent of Germany's population, they held over an eighth of professorial chairs in German universities and a quarter of the Nobel Prizes awarded to German citizens.

In a letter to the journal *Nature*, Stark argued that Germany's fight was not against its scientists, but rather against the Jews, who, in his view, had gained an inappropriate level of influence in the sciences during the Weimar years. The reform of the German civil service was not to intervene in the freedom of scientific inquiry but to restore the level of academic freedom that had existed in the past, before the establishment of the "Jewish tyranny." The Jewish scientists who had been dismissed or forced to immigrate had simply been caught up in what was really an effort to restore proper order to science in the Reich.

The Nazi campaign to eliminate Jewish professors from German universities drew a strong negative response from Jews around the world. In Stark's mind, this reaction was still further evidence of the Jewish cabal that had taken over science and that he and Lenard felt so desperately required a correction—not just in Germany but also elsewhere in Europe. For the most part, Stark aggressively enforced the law, but there were idiosyncratic exceptions where Stark personally interceded on behalf of affected Jews.

One example of Stark's unpredictable interventions was the case of Gustav Hertz. The impending dismissal was brought to Stark's attention by the German University Lecturers Association in November 1934, along with the case of Richard Gans. On Hertz's behalf, Stark ruled,

> There is nothing Jewish in Professor Hertz's outward appearance, behavior, and scientific activity. . . . He is one of our few first class German physicists and is also a Nobel Laureate. He is, in addition, the nephew of the great physicist Heinrich Hertz [with whom Lenard had studied and for whom he bore a fondness] and is thus the bearer of this famous name. It would be a blunder without parallel to deny this man the right to examine students because his grandfather was a Jew. I am convinced that he would not possibly accept such a personal insult but would resign from his office, leave the country, and be welcomed everywhere with open arms.

On the matter of Gans, Stark argued that while he "cannot boast of any accomplishments as important as those of Hertz, nevertheless, his scientific papers are of value. He also has steered clear of the Einstein circle."

It seemed at times like these that Stark was making up his own definition of who was and who was not subject to penalties under the 1933 law. At least on this particular day and for these particular supplicants, Stark saw the risk in dismissing a pair of valuable Jewish scientists. As reflected in the Gans case, an important criterion in his decision making was where a scientist stood with respect to his views of Einstein's theories. However, the dismissal of most Jewish professors did not receive this level of attention. Two years later, the Nuremburg Laws relieved both Hertz and Gans of their responsibilities to examine students, effectively removing both men from their university posts. Hertz and Gans found positions in industry. Although they were threatened by deportation to concentration camps, they ultimately were protected by their companies as essential to the war effort. Both remained in Germany throughout the war.

Relatively few German scientists truly agreed with Stark and Lenard's extreme ideological position, but it was suicidal for even the most accomplished German academics to disagree and risk drawing their predatory attention.

One example of how Stark and Lenard could place a scientist in a dangerously awkward position occurred early in Stark's administration. Stark was asked by the Ministry of Propaganda to organize a demonstration of support for Hitler by having a dozen Nobel laureates sign a brief declaration, which read, "In Adolf Hitler, we German natural researchers perceive and admire the savior and leader of the German people. Under his protection and encouragement, our scientific work will serve the German people and increase German esteem in the world." The University of Goettingen's Werner Heisenberg diplomatically responded that while he had no problem with the document itself, he felt it inappropriate for scientists to involve themselves in political affairs. The remainder of the laureates followed suit. Stark personally reported the outcome of the fiasco to Reichsminister Goebbels. Stark would not forget the embarrassment. Eventually, he would center his crosshairs directly on Heisenberg.

The behavior of the less well-known, rank-and-file, university professors proved more reliable. By removing ambitious and talented Jews from the competition, the law effectively made the path to a university job much easier for the "true Germans" who remained. Even so, Lenard's 1934 publication of *Deutsche Physik* met with general consternation in the scientific community, particularly among younger physicists who had developed the mathematical skills necessary to understand Einstein's theories.

Writing at a later time, one doctoral student wrote, "When Lenard's book, *Deutsche Physik*, was published, it met with headshaking and amazement among colleagues. We young physicists read a few pages out of curiosity, and then put it aside." The student recalled admiring one of his professors for having the courage to say, "'This is all very strange. One cannot do away with the facts of physics just like that.' We students got the message. I remember that I was glad to have this assurance and confirmation of my own thoughts."

Nevertheless, *Deutsche Physik* attracted a small but dedicated coterie of adherents whose speeches and writings proved valuable to Stark and Lenard. The 1933 civil service law had provided the leverage they needed to effectively rid German universities of Jewish professors. About twelve hundred professors from all disciplines lost their jobs in the immediate aftermath of the law's implementation. Among these were one hundred six physicists, eighty-six chemists, and eighty-five others involved in scientific investigation or the development of technology. Hundreds of others considered insufficiently supportive of the new regime were transferred to lesser positions.

All told, about sixteen hundred natural scientists summarily lost their jobs as a result of the institution of the 1933 civil service law. In the absence of any means of supporting themselves and their families, the only option for many was to leave Germany. Among them were a sampling of elite physicists, mathematicians, and chemists who eventually would assist the Allies in developing technologies that would help tip the balance of World War II against Hitler's Germany.

The scientists were part of a much larger movement. Between 1933 and 1935, enforcement of the Law for the Restoration of the Professional Civil Service caused 65,000 Jews to leave Germany. Of the remaining 562,000 Jews residing in Germany following this first wave of departures, another 300,000 emigrated because of racial or ideological discrimination. The fate of those who stayed mirrored the horrors enacted by the German armies in their sweep through Europe: 227,000 German Jews perished in concentration camps. Only a tiny enclave of 25,000 Jews remained in Germany after the war.

The emigration of German scholars did not come easily. Virtually all of the countries that might have provided safe haven had restrictive immigration policies toward Jews. In response, a number of organizations sprung up to provide money, legal assistance, and bureaucratic support for displaced German academics. Founded in London in 1933, the Academic Assistance Council had, by the end of 1935, placed sixty-two professors in tenured positions and helped one hundred forty-eight others to find at least temporary employment outside of Germany.

In 1933, the German anatomist Philipp Schwartz founded the Switzerland-based *Notgemeinschaft Deutscher Wissenschaftler*, an emergency services organization that ultimately relocated two thousand displaced German and Austrian university teachers, mostly in Great Britain and the United States. The board of the *Notgemeinschaft* was a "Who's who" of Jewish German physicists, including, at one time or another, Max Born, James Franck, and Fritz Haber. Aid societies sprung up in France and the United States as well. The American Emergency Committee in Aid of Displaced Scholars compiled lists of dismissed Jewish academics and guided as many of them as it could through often-complex processes to positions in U.S. universities. The trickle of would-be refugees quickly became a torrent, overwhelming the capacity of relief organizations to respond to the crisis.

The events in Germany, and especially his own banishment from Europe, strengthened Einstein's self-identification as a Jew. Referring back to the tumult of those times, Einstein wrote in a 1952 letter to Israeli prime minister David Ben Gurion, "My relationship to the Jewish people has become my strongest human bond ever since I became fully aware of our precarious situation among the nations of the world." Einstein had learned the hard way that his lifelong disavowal of biblical Judaism in no way exempted him from the genetic, cultural, and ethical qualities that identified him as a Jew.

Einstein gave a lecture to help raise funds for the work of the Academic Assistance Council that drew ten thousand people to London's Albert Hall. He continued his quest with Chaim Weitzmann to build what is now Hebrew University in Jerusalem and referred potential immigrant scholars to Palestine. He became personally involved in the immigration cases of his many friends and colleagues. However, over time, even Einstein's reputation could not address the demands of such a large number of dismissed German scholars. He received and responded to so many requests and wrote so many affidavits on behalf of stranded Jewish scientists that, by the late 1930s, his overused signature had lost much of its influence.

In a 1933 letter to his friend Max Born, Einstein despaired,

> Two years ago I tried to appeal to Rockefeller's conscience about the absurd method of allocating grants [to displaced scientists], unfortunately without success. Bohr has now gone to see him in an attempt to persuade him to take some action. . . . I am firmly convinced that all those who have made a name already will be taken care of. But the others, the young ones, will not have the chance to develop.

Max Born and his wife Hedi were among Einstein's closest friends, and he had conducted a regular correspondence with both of them since 1916. Like James Franck, the Borns were well-assimilated, secular Jews who had no thoughts of leaving Germany prior to the rise of Adolf Hitler. In the end, they had no choice. Stark and Lenard knew of Born's relationship with Einstein. They begrudged his support for Einstein during the events surrounding the 1920 anti-Einstein lectures at the Philharmonic and the debate at Bad Nauheim. As a friend of Einstein and a theoretical physicist to boot, Born could expect no quarter.

Born had considered following Franck's example in resigning from his post at Goettingen. However, the matter was taken out of his hands when he received a telegram on April 25, 1933, dismissing him from the faculty. Like Franck, Born had been advised that little would come of the new laws. A much-belated June 1933 letter from Werner Heisenberg, also a member of the Goettingen faculty, suggested that he and Max Planck could intervene on Born's behalf. The letter mischaracterized Planck's visit with Hitler as having been reassuring that the "Government will not undertake anything that might impede our science" and that "the political changes could take place without any damage to physics at Goettingen." Heisenberg reassured Born that "only a very few are affected by the law—certainly not you and Franck." In time, Heisenberg would personally suffer from Lenard and Stark's malevolence, but at this point he provided nothing but encouragement. He concluded, "Therefore, I entreat you not to make any decisions now but to wait to see how our country looks in the autumn."

Heisenberg had misread the tea leaves. With Stark at the helm and Lenard pulling strings with Hitler, the Nazis pursued the elimination of Jews from academic life with ever-increasing vigor. Hordes of brown shirts roamed the streets and grew more aggressive. Born became desperate about the increasing threat of violence to himself and his family. "After I had been given 'leave of absence,' we decided to leave Germany at once. We had rented an apartment for the summer vacation in Wolkenstein in the Groedner valley [of Northern Italy] . . . from a farmer by the name of Peratoner. He was willing to take us immediately. Thus, we left for the South Tyrol at the beginning of May [1933]."

The Borns and their three children became academic nomads. They first settled temporarily in Cambridge, where Born had obtained a visiting lectureship. From there, he sought Einstein's assistance in securing a permanent position while becoming involved in the quest to place other scientists who were even less fortunate than he. In June 1933, he wrote Einstein,

> Almost every week some unfortunate wretch approaches me personally, and every day I receive letters from people left stranded. And I am completely helpless, as I am myself a guest of the English and my name is not widely known;
>
> I can do nothing except advise the Academic Assistance Council in London and the *Notgemeinschaft* in Zurich. But neither of these institutions has any money.

For a while, Born held out hope that his return to Germany might be possible, but by 1934 he became convinced that he would have to find a new home and a place to work. They spent the winter of 1935–1936 in Bangalore, India, where Born was a visiting lecturer. He then spent several months lecturing in Moscow. "We were, of course, not very keen on going to Russia," he wrote, "Which would mean learning a new, very complicated language, uprooting the children a second time, and starting an entirely new life." Unable or unwilling to continue their peripatetic existence, and with no other choices available to them, the Borns applied for Russian visas and began the long process of officially becoming Russian émigrés.

In the end, Born's perseverance, his diligence in pursuing every possible opportunity, paid off. The family's wanderings ended with his recruitment to the University of Edinburgh, where Born assumed the Tait Chair of Natural Philosophy. While the post had an impressive ring to its title, there was little going on in Edinburgh in the world of theoretical physics. With little equipment and few colleagues, Born's involvement at the top level of theoretical physics came to an abrupt halt. Given the opportunities for innovative research proffered by the war effort, it was the least propitious possible time to be stuck in Edinburgh.

Seeing no way forward with his chosen career, Born reinvented himself as a scientific philosopher, an epistomologist. He cut a fresh path through the morass of conflicting arguments that had long sustained the vicious battles between Lenard's experimentalism and Einstein's theory. "A single-crystal can be clear. Nevertheless a mass of fragments of this crystal is opaque," Born noted on one occasion. "Even the theoretical physicist must be guided by the ideal of the closest possible contact with the world of facts. Only then do the formulas live and beget new life." Once stolidly aligned in the theoretical camp, Born now tried to square up the relationship between theory and observation, writing, "My advice to those who wish to learn the art of scientific prophesy is not to rely on abstract reasoning, but to decipher the secret language of Nature from Nature's documents, the facts of experience."

Born became a British citizen in 1939, the day before England entered the war against Germany. He retired to Germany in 1952. Surprisingly, his colleagues had never stopped nominating Born for a Nobel Prize, which he was awarded in 1954. The Swedish Academy of Sciences cited Born's early work on quantum mechanics, and especially his mathematical expression of the wave function. For his Nobel lecture, Born turned to the echoes of the conflict between experimental and theoretical physics.

After all, he had been in the thick of it. In his view, it was time for détente:

> I believe that ideas such as absolute certitude, absolute exactness, final truth, etc. are figments of the imagination which should not be admissible in any field of science. On the other hand, any assertion of probability is either right or wrong from the standpoint of the theory on which it is based. This loosening of thinking seems to me to be the greatest blessing which modern science has given to us. For the belief in a single truth and in being the possessor thereof is the root cause of all evil in the world.

Although Born personally did not contribute importantly to the Allies' war effort, some of the students and assistants he trained at Goettingen resided in the front rank of wartime scientists. Among his doctoral students and research assistants who immigrated to the United States and participated in the Manhattan Project were Robert Oppenheimer, Enrico Fermi, Edward Teller, and Eugene Wigner. Perhaps his most brilliant assistant, Werner Heisenberg, led the grossly underfunded and unsuccessful German effort to develop a nuclear weapon for the Third Reich. Historian Nancy Thorndike Greenspan noted that Born "let his superstars stretch past him; to those less gifted, he patiently handed out respectable but doable assignments."

The passing down of knowledge imprints something on the lineage of scholars that is as unique as the genetic imprint of families. A philosophy. A construct. A way of looking at things. Now and again, though, mutations occur. As mentioned, Born's student, Edward Teller, remains shrouded in controversy to this day. Raised in Budapest by a wealthy lawyer father and a talented pianist mother, the family was only nominally Jewish and well assimilated into Hungarian life. Teller's desire to become a mathematician clashed with his father's wish that he become an engineer. In 1926, Teller left Hungary for Karlsruhe to begin his education as a chemist. There, however, he received his first exposure to theoretical physics, a watershed in Teller's life. He loved the purity of the mathematics and the large palette of the cosmos, the backdrop on which the theorists worked. He sought and received his father's blessing to pursue his interest, but only after the elder Teller had traveled to Karlsruhe and was assured by his son's professors that Edward had the talent to succeed.

Shortly thereafter, Teller moved to Munich to work with Sommerfeld. It was in Munich that Teller was involved in a streetcar accident that severed his left foot. The accident would require him to wear a brace and walk with a pronounced limp for the rest of his life. After Munich, he was on to Leipzig and finally to Goettingen, where he attached himself to the exceptional group gathered around James Franck and Max Born.

Even though his status as a foreigner exempted Teller from the 1933 civil service law, the young man foresaw where things were headed. Germany would become a poor place for a deformed, ambitious Hungarian Jew wishing to build a career in theoretical physics. His education, training, and apprenticeships took him to London, then to Copenhagen to work for a year with Niels Bohr. By 1935, he had moved to the United States, to Washington, D.C. In 1939, he learned of experiments in Germany that showed the feasibility of a nuclear chain reaction that, if it could be controlled, would release enough energy to power a city or destroy one.

By this time, it was quite clear to all that Teller was an exceptional talent. Fermi and Szilárd brought him on to work with them on the construction of a nuclear reactor for purposes of peacetime energy. The emphasis of their work changed, however, as it began to look more likely that the United States might have to enter the war in Europe. Teller became involved in the Manhattan Project, participating at the highest level in developing a nuclear weapon.

It was when he joined the Manhattan Project that Teller became embroiled in controversy. While most of his colleagues backed the development of a fission, or so-called atomic, bomb that would make use of the German experiments, Teller felt strongly that there was an advantage in pursuing a potentially much more powerful fusion weapon, what would become better known as a hydrogen bomb. The debate brought out the darker side of Edward Teller's personality, which began to dominate his relationships with other Manhattan Project scientists. In a passive-aggressive mood, Teller was frequently late in fulfilling his responsibilities. Worse, in some cases, he simply refused to perform his assigned tasks. Teller's actions led to tensions with the other scientists, who already were irritated by his disruptive habit of playing the piano late into the night.

Teller might well have become just a footnote to the history of the development of the atomic bomb. However, in 1950, when the Soviet Union exploded its first atomic device, President Harry Truman announced that the United States would respond with an even more powerful weapon. The Cold War was on. The United States would embark on the development of a fusion bomb. The work of designing a successful hydrogen bomb fell to Edward Teller and Stanislaw Ulam. Again, controversy erupted around Teller's role in the project, in particular his calculations concerning the amount of hard-to-get tritium needed to conduct the chain reaction. Some of the scientists involved in the project believed that Teller intentionally misled supervisors by underestimating the amount of tritium needed for fear that a true assessment of the expense would terminate the project in its early stages.

Further disagreement occurred when it was time to parcel out the credit for success. "I contributed. Ulam did not," the ninety-one-year-old Teller claimed in a 1999 interview. "I'm sorry I had to answer you in this abrupt way. Ulam was rightly dissatisfied with the old approach. He came to me with a part of an idea which I already had worked out and had difficulty getting people to listen to. . . . When it then came to defending that paper and really putting work into it, he refused. He said, 'I don't believe in it.'"

Teller was not present for the detonation of "Ivy Mike," the first successful hydrogen bomb, on November 1, 1952. He told the press that he felt unwelcome. Nonetheless, he took much of the credit for the project's success. To correct what his colleagues felt was a serious public misapprehension, Fermi convinced Teller to write an article for the journal *Science* about the development of the hydrogen bomb, entitled "The Work of Many People," which appeared in February 1955. Teller later claimed that the article had been "a white lie."

Teller was a conservative "hawk" who believed the communist threat could best be addressed by the continued development of advanced weaponry. He was suspicious of colleagues who he felt were soft on Communism or who held more liberal political views. Perhaps most telling, he provoked the outrage of his colleagues by testifying against Robert Oppenheimer during the McCarthy hearings of 1954 that ultimately denied Oppenheimer further security clearance to work on government projects:

> In a great number of cases I have seen Dr. Oppenheimer act—I understood that Dr. Oppenheimer acted—in a way which for me was exceedingly hard to understand. I thoroughly disagreed with him on numerous issues and his actions frankly appeared to me confused and complicated. To this extent, I feel that I would like to see the vital interests of this country in hands which I understand better, and therefore trust more. In this very limited sense I would like to express the feeling that I would feel personally more secure if public matters would rest in other hands. . . . If it is a question of wisdom and judgment, as demonstrated by actions since 1945, then I would say one would be wiser not to grant clearance.

Enrico Fermi said of Teller that he was the only monomaniac ever to have several manias. In the end, Teller's difficulties in getting along with his colleagues, his quirks, and his rants led to him becoming something of a caricature of a mad scientist. Many believe that Teller was Stanley Kubrick's model for the crazed nuclear scientist portrayed in his 1964 satirical film, *Dr. Strangelove, or How I Learned to Stop Worrying and Love the Bomb*. In naming Teller the 1979 "honoree" of the Ig-Nobel Prizes, the sponsors of the award cited Teller's "lifelong efforts to change the meaning of peace as we know it."

Edward Teller was a brilliant mind who doubtlessly believed wholeheartedly in the strength-through-power philosophy of Ronald Reagan, whom he greatly admired. Nonetheless, his relationships with colleagues suffered through innumerable incidents, and many did not forget. Upon his death in 2003, a fellow Manhattan Project scientist and Nobel laureate, Isidor Rabi, whose family had immigrated to the United States when he was a child, said, "I do really feel it would have been a better world without Teller."

13

SOME SAY BY FIRE, OTHERS ICE

The secretary knocked softly and waited until he heard a response before opening the door. He leaned forward just enough to insert his head past the jam to tell SS Reichsfuehrer Heinrich Himmler that his mother was in the outer office. Should he escort her in? Himmler's impatience sent the young man scurrying back to his desk. But by the time Himmler greeted his "Mutti," his attitude had changed dramatically. In less than a minute, he had regressed forty years, back to his childhood when pleasing "Mutti" had dominated his thoughts.

Growing up in Bavaria, Himmler's nondescript, nebbish appearance, social awkwardness, lack of athletic ability, and rigid obedience had earned him plaudits from his teachers and the scorn of his schoolmates. As an adult, these same qualities had brought him political power far beyond even his mother's fevered imaginings. At home in the Munich headquarters of the SS, he was admired for his cool efficiency and feared for the absence of any hint of human compassion. In the presence of his staunchly devout Roman Catholic mother, though, he was a different man. With a desperation he'd never managed to resolve in childhood, an empty place in his heart still sought her approval of his accomplishments and attention to her desires.

Despite how close he was to his mother, it was unusual for Mutti to visit him at work. He considered asking her outright why she had stopped by but thought better of it. There was a ritual order to their conversations as inalterable as High Mass. He listened as she fussed over his health. Was he getting enough sleep? Eating properly? Even the state of his bowels was a matter of motherly interest. He was used to this. He courteously submitted to her interrogation and waited.

Quite nonchalantly, several minutes into their conversation, his mother mentioned that she had received an unexpected visit from a distant friend of the family. Did he remember Annie Heisenberg. No? Well, she wasn't sure. Perhaps they had never met. Annie was the wife of August Heisenberg. Mr. Heisenberg and Mutti's father, Grandpapa Heyder, had both been teachers, rectors of their schools, and knew each other from their hiking club. Annie's son, Werner, was in some kind of trouble. She wouldn't ordinarily have bothered her Heinrich except that, as a mother, she could identify with her friend's concerns.

Annie had told her that poor Werner had been the subject of a very unfavorable article in the SS weekly publication, *Das Schwarze Korps*. At first, Annie had dismissed it as nothing, but the more she thought about it, the more afraid she became. After all, there had been an earlier attack. She thought it had been written by a man named Menzel. Yes. She was almost certain that his name was Menzel. Would Heinrich please humor her and see what he could do to help her friend's son?

Himmler was well aware that Werner Heisenberg was under fire. He had met the Nobel Prize–winning physicist on several occasions and found him to be a typical academic with his head in the clouds. Still, he was considered to be the most prominent scientist remaining in Germany now that the law reforming the civil service and the Nuremberg laws had flushed the Jews from the universities. With the Jews out of the way, Lenard and Stark had turned their attention to the "white Jews," theoretical physicists like Heisenberg whom they viewed as improperly influenced by Albert Einstein.

Himmler refocused his attention on his mother's voice. She had moved on to other topics, but it was this visit by Heisenberg's mother that had been the reason for her decision to stop by and speak with her son. Several minutes later, after once again admonishing her Heinrich to take care of his health, she voiced the traditional Bavarian benediction, *Gruess Gott*, and left.

Himmler had his secretary bring him the SS's files on Werner Heisenberg. What a mess this fellow had gotten himself into. For someone generally acknowledged to be a genius, he was not very smart at all. He had been swimming against the tide for years, flaunting his admiration of Einstein, Bohr, and other discredited theoreticians in the face of the Nazis' new dialectic.

Himmler opened a packet of newspaper clippings. Johannes Stark had set his cat's paw, a student named Willi Menzel, to author a propaganda piece for a January 1936 edition of *Voelkischer Beobachter*. Skimming quickly, several items caught Himmler's attention: "theoreticians like Einstein . . . propagated their ideas in the manner characteristic of Jews and forced them upon physicists . . . ridicule men who criticized this new type of 'science' . . . the lofty spheres of the Einsteinian intellect."

Further down, Menzel cited Lenard's *Deutsche Physik* and lauded Lenard for "single-handedly" having held the proper name "German" above the adjective "Jewish." The article closed with a battle cry: "We, the younger generation want to continue the fight today for German physics; and we will succeed in elevating its name to the same heights that German technology and science has already been enjoying for a long time."

It was the usual propaganda, Himmler thought. Acceptance of the principles of *Deutsche Physik* had been a good litmus test for scientists' allegiance to the Reich. Although Stark had proven a terrible administrator, full of grandiose plans that he would never be able to implement, Himmler couldn't fault either Lenard or Stark for their enthusiasm. Nonetheless, watching the two scientists buffalo their colleagues into their way of thinking had made him cynical of their actual motives.

Heisenberg had played the fool. He should have known better than to respond to this pap. Publishing Menzel's article had been an obvious trap, baited by Lenard and Stark to irk Heisenberg into publicly airing his impolitic views. Amazingly, Heisenberg had failed to recognize the danger. Just look at what he had written!

Ignoring Menzel, whom he considered merely a ghost writer, Heisenberg directed his readers to the true perpetrators: "On the authority of Ph. Lenard and J. Stark, two of the most senior and meritorious German physicists, W. Menzel offers arguments against theoretical physics . . . that appear erroneous and misleading to the majority of younger scientists." Heisenberg adopted a paternalistic style, writing, "A serious analysis of this changed situation leads the exact sciences away from the naïve materialistic conception of the world." In concluding, Heisenberg responded to Menzel's challenge with one of his own. "The continuation of this research, which may well exert the greatest influence on the structure of our intellectual life as a whole, is one of the noblest missions of German youth in science."

The newspaper had preceded Heisenberg's words with a disclaimer: "Since we can by no means agree with the views expressed in this [Heisenberg's] reply, we have turned to Professor Stark as an authority in the field of physics, asking him his opinion, which is printed subsequently."

Doubtlessly, this had been the plan all along. Once Heisenberg had displayed his true stripes, Stark would get the last word. Himmler knew without looking what Stark must have written. He knew what he would've done; he wasn't disappointed.

"For clarity's sake," Stark began, "It is essential that the preceding article by Heisenberg be rectified immediately. It is designed to give the impression to readers who are not physics experts that the great discoveries in physics of recent decades were an achievement of theory, and wherever possible even of Jewish theory."

Stark depicted the whole of theoretical physics as a Jewish lie. It had not been theory but "careful observation and measurement by experimental physicists" that had led Germany to supremacy in the natural sciences. True Germans had discovered, for example, X-rays, radioactivity, and the effect of magnetic fields on spectral lines. "No productive experimental physicist," he wrote, "uses Einstein's relativity theories as a point of departure for research." In the end, Stark took advantage of the opportunity Heisenberg had afforded him to paint the talented young physicist with the tarred brush of Judaism:

In his article, Heisenberg continues to advocate the fundamental attitude of Jewish physics even today. Indeed, he even expects that young Germans should adopt this basic attitude and take Einstein and his comrades as their models in science. . . . The article by the student Menzel is a welcome sign that young Germans are shunning the influence of Jewish physics and that they want to study physics in the same spirit that pervades Lenard's recently published textbook, *Deutsche Physik*, which reflects physical reality without "the new systems of concepts."

If only Heisenberg hadn't stuck his neck out, Himmler thought as he turned to the last newspaper article in the file, the recent article in *Das Schwarze Korps* that Mutti had mentioned, the one entitled "White Jews in Science." He noticed immediately that there was no byline; Stark had hidden behind a cloak of anonymity. No matter. Stark's rhetoric was unmistakable. Again, he skimmed the text, retaining snapshots of the content:

. . . primitive type of anti-Semitism that limits itself to fighting against Jews alone. . . .
. . . not dealing with Jews per se, but rather with the mentality, or rather bad mentality, they spread. . . .
When the carrier of this mentality is not a Jew but a German. . . .
. . . could also speak of Jews in spirit, of Jews by mentality.
. . . intellectual ties of white Jews to Jewish role models and masters.

All of this was well-worn, vintage Lenard. Stark in full rant. The pair of them had an insatiable appetite for Jew-baiting. But there was something new. This article named names. He slowed down and read more carefully:

The Jews Einstein, Haber, and their mind mates, Sommerfeld and Planck. Had they been allowed to have their way, in a few decades, the type of scientist that is productive and close to reality would have died out. National Socialism's seizure of power has staved off this danger.

Himmler knew as well as Stark that Sommerfeld and Planck were both old and revered. They were untouchable. Their mention was merely Stark's way of getting to his true target, Heisenberg.

> How secure 'white Jews' feel in their positions is evidenced by the actions of the professor for theoretical physics in Leipzig, Professor Werner Heisenberg, who . . . declared Einstein's relativity theory to be the obvious 'basis for further research' and saw 'one of the noblest missions of German youth in science as the continued development of theoretical systems of concepts.

Nor had Stark forgotten an old slight that had made him look impotent to the Nazi leadership:

> Heisenberg returned his thanks in August 1934 by refusing to sign a proclamation by the German Nobel Laureates for his support of the Fuehrer and Chancellor. His response then was, 'Although I personally vote 'yes,' political declarations by scientists seem to me improper, since this was never a normal practice even formerly. Therefore, I do not sign'. . . . This response exemplifies the Jewish mentality of its author. . . . Heisenberg is only one example among several others. All of them are puppets of Jewry in German intellectual life and must disappear, just as the Jews themselves.

The last paragraph called upon Johannes Stark to comment on its contents, as though he'd had nothing to do with instigating the article to begin with. In his commentary, Stark acknowledged the wisdom of the *Das Schwarze Korps* article in his opening sentences: "The preceding article is basically so appropriate and complete that further additions would really be superfluous." However, his approval did not stop him from inscribing another five hundred words on his favorite themes.

Himmler had read enough to know that things had gotten out of hand. Left to their own devices, Lenard and Stark's rhetoric might get Heisenberg killed by some crazed storm trooper or, worse, run him out of Germany where another country might pick him up. He would have to call off Stark and his aged mentor, Philipp Lenard, at least until he decided how to handle this affair. He would be in a bind no matter how things turned out. War was coming, and they would need Heisenberg's brain, but if his office simply ignored the situation, he'd have Stark at his door. Not to mention Mutti. As though he didn't already have enough to do without inserting himself into the petty squabbles of scientists!

The heat on Himmler turned up a notch when, just five days after the original article was published in *Das Schwarze Korps*, a letter dated July 20, 1937, from a University of Leipzig colleague of Heisenberg's, Friedrich Hund, turned up at the offices of Reichminister for Science, Education, and National Culture Bernhard Rust. The letter complained of Stark's "abusive statements" about Heisenberg "that exceeded all bounds of decency." The author closed his letter with "I have confidence that you, Mister Reichminister, will prevent the President of the Reich Physical and Technical Institute from injuring the honor of our science any further in this matter."

Luckily, much of the decision concerning what to do about Heisenberg was taken out of Himmler's hands by Heisenberg himself. On July 21, 1937, Heisenberg wrote directly to Himmler demanding either Himmler's approval of Stark's attacks or that he lodge an objection with Stark and warn him not to engage in future attacks. He further requested that he undergo a formal investigation of the charges made in the sequence of articles appearing in *Das Schwarze Korps*.

Himmler thought Heisenberg's suggestion an excellent idea and conducted his investigation with a vengeance. He had three members of his personal staff—all former students of physics—install microphones in Heisenberg's home and attend his lectures at Leipzig University. On several occasions, Heisenberg was brought to Gestapo headquarters to undergo daylong interrogations that left him shaken. The investigators spent an inordinate amount of time on Heisenberg's sexuality. It was rumored that the married scientist was a homosexual, a crime under Nazi law, punishable by imprisonment in a concentration camp.

Exactly one year to the day, July 21, 1938, Himmler wrote two letters that settled the issue. One letter he sent to SS Gruppenfuehrer Reinhard Heydrich, essentially saying that Germany could not afford to lose or silence Heisenberg, as he was necessary to the education of a generation of scientists. The other letter was a personal note to Heisenberg:

> I have had your case examined with particular care and scrutiny, since you are recommended to me by my family. I am happy to be able to inform you today that I do not approve of the offensive article by Das Schwarze Korps and that I have put a stop to any further attacks on you. I hope that I can see you at my office in Berlin someday in the autumn—though only very late, in November or December—so that we can have a man-to-man talk about this.

Himmler signed the letter "With friendly greetings and Heil Hitler!" and added a postscript: "I do find it appropriate, though, that in the future you separate clearly for your students acknowledgment of scientific research results from the scientist's personal and political views." Going forward, Heisenberg was to make a point about the source of the information he'd imparted and advise his students of the source's standing from the perspective of the Third Reich.

It was ironic that Stark had gone after Heisenberg based on the younger man's relationship with Einstein. Although Heisenberg's work owed much to Einstein's, the two were somewhat distant with each other and never resolved fundamental differences in key conceptions of theoretical physics. Heisenberg later recalled a conversation he'd had with Einstein concerning the role that theory played in the progress of science. In a conversation about the structure of the atom following Einstein's attendance at a lecture that Heisenberg delivered in 1926 at the University of Berlin, Einstein invited Heisenberg to walk with him. Years later, Heisenberg remembered what they'd discussed:

> **Heisenberg**: Since a good theory must be based on directly observable magnitudes, I thought it more fitting to restrict myself to these [observations of emitted radiation], treating them, as it were, as representatives of electron orbits.

> **Einstein**: But you don't seriously believe that none but observable magnitudes must go into a physical theory?

Heisenberg: Isn't that precisely what you have done with relativity?

Einstein: Possibly I did use this kind of reasoning, but it is nonsense all the same. . . . It is quite wrong to try founding a theory on observable magnitudes alone. . . . It is the theory which decides what we can observe.

In essence, Heisenberg was drawing his arguments from the experimentalists, albeit in a much more civilized manner than Lenard or Stark, neither of whom was prone to mannerly subtleties.

In taking stock of what had transpired between Stark and Heisenberg, it was clear to Himmler that Stark had not progressed with the times. Stark presented several specific liabilities that he could no longer abide. First, he was an unrepentant ideologue who unfailingly seemed to make enemies. An internal SS report commissioned by Himmler found that although Stark was philosophically aligned with the National Socialist movement, he was politically inept. His insistence on fostering only research that met his own tightly circumscribed criteria too often ran afoul of the pragmatic needs of the state. To Himmler, good research was research that served the interests of the Reich.

Moreover, Stark failed to recognize the importance to Himmler of his own special interest in research. Himmler was a devotee of the occult. He had been pursuing evidence in support of the "world ice theory," which hypothesized that modern-day Aryans were descendants of an ancient Aryan culture that had ruled the world. Himmler had incorporated into the SS a research division known as *Forschungsgemeinschaft Deutsches Ahnenerbe*, which had commissioned several expeditions to Germany, Finland, and Sweden to conduct archeological and anthropological investigations that Himmler felt would support his contentions.

Karl Weigel, a member of Himmler's *Ahnenerbe* research group, requested funding from Stark's German Research Fund for an *Ahnenerbe* project. Stark rejected the proposal, arguing that *Ahnenerbe* was "unscientific." The ensuing SS report was forwarded to Himmler. Himmler interpreted Stark's failure to demonstrate any understanding of, take an interest in, or have his research fund sponsor projects dealing with Himmler's theories as a rejection of Himmler's beliefs.

Stark also had other failings that now made him a target. He had never enjoyed the support of German scientists, to whom he appeared power hungry and overbearing. Several years previously, the responsibility for overseeing scientific research had been transferred from the highly supportive Reichminister Wilhelm Frick to Bernhard Rust, with whom Stark had previously scuffled. Perhaps for some inadvertent slight or simply for the thrill of the intrigue at the highest levels of German government, Rust claimed that Stark had made derogatory comments about the Reich's scientific policies to outsiders, and as punishment halved his research budget.

Perhaps most significantly, Stark had a way of sticking his nose where it didn't belong. He had gotten himself into considerable trouble by calling for the punishment of a local National Socialist official who had been convicted of embezzlement, which ran afoul of a powerful regional party official. Unwittingly, Stark had violated a party rule concerning jurisdiction. The Nazi Party took him to court, calling for his dismissal. Although ultimately an appeals court refused to progress to trial in recognition of Stark's early support of Adolf Hitler, Stark was humiliated.

In the end, even his friends in the party turned on him. Alfred Rosenberg no longer published his articles in *Voelkischer Beobachter*, nor were his opinions welcome in *Das Schwarze Korps*. A major pet project failed miserably. He had invested a great deal of the Reich's money in a misguided scheme to alchemically turn peat hewn from the swamps of southern Germany into gold. To avoid this chicanery coming to light, he was required to "voluntarily" step down from his post with the German Research Fund. In Stark's mind, the concatenation of events proved what he had known all along: there was a conspiracy against him.

Most of Germany's natural scientists watched the demise of Stark and Lenard's influence with satisfaction. The pair had made few friends during their time lording over the natural sciences, and Stark's interpretation of the Fuehrer Principle had quashed debate. *Deutsche Physik* became a terminal footnote to what, before the civil service law, had been a remarkable flowering of German science. The few remaining advocates of *Deutsche Physik* were silenced. In 1940, National Socialist leadership called for the recognition of relativity theory and quantum mechanics as acceptable bases for scientific work. Lenard's twenty-year fight against Einstein, the man, and his far-reaching theories finally was over. His influence at an end, the long-retired professor faded into obscurity. War was coming. War demanded a more pragmatic approach to scientific investigation.

Stark returned to his family estate in rural Bavaria, where he suffered the aftereffects of his disillusionment with the Nazi bureaucracy. Still a target of retribution for his many enemies, Stark's son Hans was arrested by the Gestapo on a trumped-up charge of being too kind to a Polish slave laborer and was sent to the Eastern front. When Stark tried to resign from the National Socialist Party, local officials forced him to remain a Nazi by making further threats upon his son's life. Toward the end of the war, Stark's rural estate was taken over by an SS officer who eventually gave way to the occupation of the American military.

In 1945, Stark was arrested by the Allied authorities. He faced trial for war crimes. In court, old enmities came home to roost. Max von Laue, Werner Heisenberg, and Arnold Sommerfeld all testified against him. From the other side of the Atlantic, Einstein submitted written testimony that Stark had been "a highly egocentric person with an unusually high craving for recognition . . . [and a] paranoid personality." On June 20, 1947, a tribunal found Johannes Stark guilty, and classified him as bearing major guilt (*Hauptschuldiger*). Despite being over seventy years old, he was sentenced to four years at hard labor.

The appeals process reversed the initial verdict, downgrading his offenses to those of a "follower." According to the appeals court, Stark had "never acted unilaterally to cause damage to non-National Socialists among his colleagues" and that "his ideological advocacy for National Socialism had never led to condemnable actions." He paid a fine of 1,000 marks and was freed.

In their prime, Philipp Lenard and Johannes Stark had experienced something close to absolute power over the German scientific community. They had held in their hands the lives of tens of thousands and almost without exception had used their authority for ill. Their decline was abrupt and painful, all the more so because they failed to see their own complicity in the factors that had led to their fall. They had been active participants in the era of Nazism. By their mindless adherence to a philosophical belief in the superiority of one race over another, they caused irreparable harm to countless lives and, ultimately, had much to do with the decimation of their own country.

EPILOGUE: UNAPOLOGETIC LIVES

Gingerly grasping the nail between his right thumb and forefinger, Philipp Lenard tapped his hammer tentatively at first, then with a bit more vigor. He tested the nail to be certain that it held firmly in the whitewashed plaster. Bent with age, his arms restricted by the tight-fitting dark suit he had donned for his birthday portrait earlier in the day, he turned to lift from his desk a framed photograph. His hands shook as he raised it high and looped the frame's braided wire hanger over the nail. He took a step backward to improve his perspective before alternately sliding the dark wood frame left and right until it was perfectly aligned, top and bottom parallel with the ceiling.

Lenard gazed at the image, soaking in every detail as though he feared it might vanish. The portrait depicted a powerful visage caught, seemingly unaware, in a serious contemplative moment. The Fuehrer's eyes stared intently from the base of a high, smooth brow. Lenard knew, firsthand, the eyes to be a brilliant piercing blue and how unnerving it could be to stare into their unblinking intensity. Beneath the distinctive nose sat the small swath of hair that had become so recognizable as to become fodder for caricature. The professor smiled his old man's smile, further deepening the furrows that lined his face. He was eighty years old that day. What a remarkable surprise. He could not have imagined a better gift.

Lenard seated himself at his desk, but only for an instant. Unable to contain his excitement, he grasped his cane and pushed himself halfway out of his chair to scrutinize once more the signature in the lower corner of the portrait. The Fuehrer, himself, had signed it. He glanced again at the image. To Lenard, the pathos in the Fuehrer's expression expressed all that need be said. He had sacrificed everything, even gone to prison, to restore the Fatherland to its rightful place, chief among nations. Lenard experienced a frisson of pleasure, imagining that at this very moment, perhaps, the Fuehrer's armies were exacting harsh retribution upon those who had unfairly humbled the German people following the Great War.

Lenard turned his attention to the large, khaki-colored envelope that had arrived by courier earlier in the day. If the Fuehrer had sent only the photograph, that would have been ecstasy. But, in fact, there had been a letter too. A personal letter from the Fuehrer. He wiped his fingers on his fine wool trousers before laying his hands on the letter. Skimming the contents, Lenard came quickly to the words that, despite his having read them several times, still dizzied him with their praise. "With you, the National Socialists' thoughts have had a courageous supporter and brave fighter since the beginning, who effectively curtailed the Jewish influence on science and who always has been my faithful and appreciated colleague. This shall never be forgotten."

Lenard nodded. He had supported the National Socialist's cause long before the politics of the times demanded it. In retrospect, he had been impetuous. But when the Nazis came to power, the gamble paid off. The party awarded Lenard its highest honors. After his retirement in 1932, the Reich had immortalized him by naming for him the Institute of Physics at the University of Heidelberg, where he had been the director for most of his career. The Philipp Lenard Institute, he thought, and nearly spoke the words aloud.

Grand as these accolades were, the professor felt there had been something lacking. The public had not loved him in the same way it had favored other scientists, even those of lesser accomplishment. He had never escaped his deep disappointment in the scant public recognition his discoveries had garnered. Receiving the Nobel Prize for his work describing the emanations of cathode ray tubes had been the zenith. But even then, neither his colleagues nor the masses had properly acknowledged the importance of his contributions. He had been in the thick of *so many* discoveries. Without so much as a nod in his direction, covetous charlatans and fame seekers had stolen the credit that rightfully was his.

He picked up his pen, writing on the inner leaf of the 1935 program for the inauguration of the Philipp Lenard Institute of Physics in Heidelberg, "I was repeatedly honored; my thinking, however, was not observed. I have rebelled against such nonsense for six years. Now, as I am eighty years old, I have become too old to further come into action, as has already been the case with my writings."

How had he become so old? Even the exertion of writing discomfited him. He stretched his neck against the constricting dark tie and starchstiff collar that bit into his thin, old man's skin. The Fuehrer had put his finger on the problem—"the Jewish influence." The Jews had duped his Aryan colleagues into believing their degenerate theorics. Together, they had cheated him of his proper place in the pantheon of great scientists. The misplaced public fuss over the white Jew, Roentgen, had been a prime example. Roentgen, the famous Wuerzburg professor. Lenard well knew that Roentgen was not a Jew, but it was as though he were. He had been a friend of Jews, and he had thought like one. Roentgen had somehow blundered into perceiving the existence of X-rays. He had blithely accepted the credit as though his discovery had leapt from some wellspring of scientific sorcery, as though Lenard had not spent years laying out the fundamental groundwork. The world was so unfair. Without Lenard's signal contributions, the world would never have heard the name of Wilhelm Conrad Roentgen. It still rankled that Roentgen died never having acknowledged Lenard's role as the true "mother of the X-ray." The Reich corrected that oversight, belatedly crediting Lenard with the discovery, but it had held little meaning. It came too late. Consumed by war, the world took little notice.

Lenard returned his attention to the letter. The business with Roentgen had been largely a private matter. Hitler was thinking of something entirely different when he penned his reference to "the Jewish influence."

Einstein. The charlatan and his great Jewish fraud, the theory of relativity. Einstein had posed a much greater threat. The Jew and his claims for his theories of relativity stood in opposition to the essence of Lenard's *Deutsche Physik*, to the superiority of Aryan physics. The ludicrous public comparisons of Einstein's theories to the works of the greatest scientific thinkers of the past mocked the Aryan spirit. Lenard's dealings with Einstein had been his greatest trial. In testament, he had written, "If I had known that mankind would run itself down so badly during my lifetime, that man would degrade from Friedrich the Great to Friedrich Ebert, from Newton to Einstein, I would have never resolved in my youth to serve the best men of my time."

Absorbed in his memories, Lenard fumed over how little credit he had received for his courageous stance. Had he not stood up to Einstein and called him to account, who can say what might have happened? He had exposed the Jew to his colleagues for the sham that he was. He had risked his own career and, given the power the Jew commanded, perhaps even his life. But he had put the Jew on the defensive.

Although it was not until 1933 that the Jew fled Germany with a price on his head, Lenard had been in the vanguard. Einstein had been fortunate to get out when he did. His flight to England, then on to America, had almost certainly saved him from an early death. With Einstein gone, he'd led the purge that, in short order, eliminated the duplicitous Jewish race from German academic life.

That Hitler had remembered Lenard's contributions and so fulsomely expressed his gratitude gave renewed meaning to the aged professor's constricted life. The Fuehrer knew more than anyone about sacrifice, yet here he was acknowledging the hardships Lenard had suffered. The struggle had been worthwhile.

While Lenard's grudges would dog him until his death five years later in Messelhausen, Germany, the good feelings of that day in 1942 never completely left him. Unrepentant of the harm he had caused to so many people and certain that his assessment of Einstein and his theories had been correct, he sat alone in his room, Hitler's visage watching over him, and reflected with satisfaction on the experiences that had brought him to his place in the world. Waxing philosophical, Lenard lifted his pen and wrote in the stilted style of one born in a distant province who, from childhood, had scorned all learning but science, "To have Adolf Hitler and to know him close to me should be enough to have lived for."

* * *

"I have done my share." Einstein said. Lying in his hospital bed, he painfully turned toward his longtime secretary, Helen Dukas. "It is time to go. I will do it elegantly."

Einstein had been admitted to Princeton Hospital several hours earlier, on April 17, 1955, complaining of chest pain that had worsened over the last several days. Einstein's premonition of his death was well founded. Seven years earlier, in 1948, doctors discovered that he had developed a "grapefruit-size" aneurysm of the aorta, the body's largest artery. Nowadays, localized vascular balloonings like Einstein's are routinely treated by surgery or radiological procedures. At that time, however, surgical methods for treating aneurysms were more rudimentary. Einstein's physicians felt that there was too much risk for them to operate. Now the aneurysm was leaking, causing pain, signaling it would soon burst.

Having refused emergency surgery, the seventy-six-year-old made himself as comfortable as he could. He reminded Dukas that he wished to be cremated the day he died. She and his older son, Hans Albert, were to spread his ashes on the waters of the Delaware River, just to the west of where he had lived and worked for the past twenty-two years. There should be no memorial service and no marker to commemorate his passing.

Between his admission to the hospital and his death early the next morning, Einstein had several hours to contemplate the cosmic questions that had occupied him during his remarkably fruitful life. Einstein had been born to Jewish parents. He bore no illusions, however, concerning the meaning of being a Jew. Recent history had made it clear to him that "A Jew who sheds his faith along the way, or who even picks up a different one, is still a Jew." The Nazi's near extermination of European

Jewry and his efforts to establish a Jewish university in Jerusalem had strengthened his identification with Judaism as he'd aged. His beliefs, however, were his own:

> I cannot imagine a God who rewards and punishes the objects of his creation, whose purposes are modeled after our own—a God, in short, who is but a reflection of human frailty. Neither can I believe that the individual survives the death of his body. . . . It is enough for me to contemplate the mystery of conscious life perpetuating itself through all eternity, to reflect upon the marvelous structure of the universe which we can dimly perceive, and to try humbly to comprehend even an infinitesimal part of the intelligence manifested in nature. My religion consists of a humble admiration of the illimitable superior spirit who reveals himself in the slight details we are able to perceive with our frail and feeble minds.

Einstein died early in the morning on April 18, 1955. He was seventy-six years old. There was no deathbed conversion. He remained true to his convictions in death, as he had in life.

Throughout the United States and around the world, people whom Einstein had never met mourned his passing. The loss was particularly heartfelt in Princeton. The locals had grown accustomed to seeing Einstein, dressed in baggy trousers, a rumpled sweater, and sandals, on his daily walks around the town. Despite his once having voiced the opinion that Princeton was a "quaint and ceremonial village of puny demigods, strutting on stiff legs," he loved the small college town's deep, green leafiness and the stone spires of its renowned university from the moment he arrived. He quickly renegotiated his position with the Institute for Advanced Studies from being a five-or-six months a year visiting scholar to a year-round member of its faculty. In 1934, he and Elsa bought an ordinary-looking house at 112 Mercer Street and moved in along with Helen Dukas and, later, after Elsa's untimely death in 1936, Elsa's daughter Margot.

Local anecdotes are legion and almost always sympathetic. Among them is a story about two undergraduates who saw Einstein walking ahead of them on campus one day and conspired to get his attention.

"One plus one equals two!" one of them said in a voice loud enough for Einstein to hear. "You're an idiot . . . you know that?" said the other. "One plus one equals three!" The argument grew more voluble until, after a minute or so, Einstein stopped abruptly and turned to face them. "Boys, boys," he admonished them. "There is no need to fight. You are both right!"

Other stories describe him as an eccentric, seemingly so deeply absorbed in the enormity of his thoughts that he was incapable of managing the mundane aspects of normal life. One such story was told by an undergraduate returning to campus in late summer, just before the beginning of the academic year. The young man decided to spend his otherwise unencumbered afternoon canoeing on Lake Carnegie at the foot of the campus. Only one other boat was on the water, a becalmed sailboat that at first glance seemed to be unmanned. As the young man approached the boat, a man and a woman raised themselves above the gunwales and waved him over. The man's disarrayed shock of white hair left no doubt to his identity. Einstein had forgotten to put a paddle in the boat. They had been dead in the water for over an hour. Would the young man tow them to port?

The woman in the boat almost certainly was Polish-born Johanna Fantiva, Einstein's last lover, whom he had convinced to immigrate to Princeton in 1939. Twenty-two years younger than Einstein, she left a diary in which much is written about a man quite different than the muddle-headed genius of township lore. Johanna characterized Einstein as an extremely alert and keen-witted critic of his time, angered by Senator McCarthy's anti-communist campaign, the U.S.-supported rearming of Germany, and the American buildup of atomic weapons. In Johanna's diary, Einstein comes alive as an amiable maverick who compared himself to an old car, rife with mechanical problems. Despite his ills, Fantiva asserted that he not only retained his own good humor but also cheered up his chronically depressed parrot, Bibo, by telling him jokes.

By the time Einstein reached Princeton, he was fifty-four years old. His best science was behind him, but he remained among the most respected men on the planet. He had lived his life according to a consistent

moral code. While many disagreed with his message of pacifistic internationalism, even his critics had to grant that Einstein had stayed true to his
credo. He had seen enough of prejudice and ostracism that he would not
stand for it in any form. He developed a particular empathy for the plight
of black people in America. He was a longtime friend of the actor Paul
Robeson, who had grown up in Princeton. When the great African-
American opera singer Marian Anderson was denied lodging at Princeton's Nassau Inn following a 1937 performance, he invited her into his
home. From then on, she stayed with Einstein whenever she was in the
area.

Unfortunately, Einstein's comfort with his pacifist beliefs was challenged by events happening overseas. He fearfully monitored the increasingly bellicose speeches of Adolf Hitler and recognized that Europe once
again was heading toward war. During the summer of 1939, while Einstein was vacationing in Peconic, on the northern tip of Long Island, he
welcomed to his rental cottage two old friends. Eugene Wigner and Leó
Szilárd were Hungarian refugees and physicists, who had managed to
escape Europe before Hitler had tightened the noose around that country's scientists.

Greeting the two men in an undershirt and rolled-up trousers, he led
them to the screened-in porch where he listened to their story. Their visit
was not a social one. Wigner and Szilárd had received word that German
physicists had learned how to split the uranium atom. As Einstein had
predicted in his 1905 work on the equivalence of mass and energy—
represented by his iconic formula, energy (E) equals mass (m) multiplied
by the speed of light (c) squared, or $E = mc^2$—the reaction released an
enormous amount of energy. Werner Heisenberg was said to be leading a
German effort to build an atomic bomb. Time was short. Einstein must
use his influence to prevail on his friend Elisabeth, Belgium's former
Queen—now Queen Mother following the death of her husband—to have
her country deny Germany access to the great stores of uranium in the
Belgian Congo.

Einstein agreed, but before he could write the letter, Szilárd was convinced by a friend of President Roosevelt that any international effort

would be advantaged by their going through government channels. Szilárd returned to Long Island, this time with another Hungarian refugee, the eventual father of the hydrogen bomb, Edward Teller, in tow.

Einstein knew Roosevelt personally, having been invited with Elsa to have dinner with the president and Mrs. Roosevelt and spend the night at the White House in 1934. At Szilárd and Teller's urging, he dictated a letter to Roosevelt dated August 2, 1939. Because of the demands of the presidency, however, Roosevelt didn't learn of Einstein's concerns until early October, when his friend and economic advisor Alexander Sachs finally read Einstein's letter aloud to the president.

In barebones fashion, Einstein's missive provided Roosevelt with the background he felt the president needed to understand the magnitude of the crisis and how researchers had come to unleash the power of the atom. He went on to express his concern that "[t]his new phenomenon would also lead to the construction of bombs [and] . . . that extremely powerful bombs of a new type may thus be constructed." He warned, "A single bomb of this type, carried by a boat and exploded in a port might very well destroy the whole port, together with some of the surrounding territory."

In light of the fact that the United States then had very sparse known stores of uranium, and that German scientists might be well on their way to weaponizing this new threat, Einstein suggested that the president "have some permanent contact maintained between the Administration and the group of physicists working on chain reactions in America." Einstein envisioned that this unnamed individual would keep government departments informed and facilitate special attention to the availability of uranium, as well as advise the government on increasing funding to universities and institutes so as to accelerate research on nuclear fission.

It took some time, but Roosevelt eventually treated Einstein's warning seriously. He established a board that included members of his military command, as well as Szilárd, Wigner, Teller, and the physicist Enrico Fermi, who had escaped Mussolini's fascist Italy. Einstein was invited to join the following year, but declined and later was excluded for reasons of national security.

When, in 1933, Einstein first determined he would immigrate, his entry into the United States was opposed by an organization billing itself as the Women's Patriot Corporation. This group had charged that Einstein's associations with a number of European pacifist organizations identified him as a communist. The memoranda of that episode of back and forth with the U.S. government had been retained in what, over the years, had grown to become a fourteen-hundred-page FBI file. FBI Director J. Edgar Hoover claimed that Einstein was an "extreme radical." Hoover's judgment effectively ruled out Einstein's participation in the Manhattan Project.

In warning Roosevelt of the German threat and advocating work on nuclear fission weaponry, Einstein had envisioned nuclear weapons as a deterrent or, at worst, weapons that would only be used defensively. He was devastated by the catastrophic loss of life that resulted at Hiroshima and Nagasaki. At the urging of Szilárd, who was similarly troubled, he assumed the presidency of a new organization, the Emergency Committee of Atomic Scientists, dedicated to nuclear arms control, and rededicated himself to the impossible chimera of a unified world government.

Einstein spent most of his last years in Princeton working on a "unified field theory"—a scientific and mathematical construct that would comprehensively explain the interrelationships among all natural phenomena. In the end, the conquest of this last great challenge eluded him. Nonetheless, Einstein died believing that such an understanding was achievable. "The most incomprehensible thing about the world," he wrote, "is that it is comprehensible."

BIBLIOGRAPHY

All Web sites were last accessed September 5, 2014.

A NOTE ON THE DIFFERENCES BETWEEN LENARD'S AND EINSTEIN'S SCIENCE

Kostro, L. (2000). *Einstein and the ether*. Montreal: Apeiron.

Lacayo, R., & Editors of *Time*. (2014). *Albert Einstein: The enduring legacy of a modern genius*. New York: Time.

Relativity. Retrieved from http://en.wikipedia.org/wiki/Relativity

CHAPTER 1: PYRRHIC VICTORY

Albert Einstein. Retrieved from http://en.wikipedia.org/wiki/Albert_Einstein

Ash, M. G., & Sollner, A. (1996). *Forced migration and scientific change: Émigré German-speaking scientists and scholars after 1933*. Berlin: German Historical Institute.

Bentwish, N. (1953). *Rescue and achievement of refugee scholars: The story of displaced scholars and scientists, 1933–1952*. The Hague: Martinus Nijhoff.

Dukas, H., & Hoffmann, B. (1979). *Albert Einstein: The human side*. Princeton, NJ: Princeton University Press.

Elisabeth of Bavaria, Queen of Belgium. Retrieved from http://en.wikipedia.org/wiki/Elisabeth_of_Bavaria_(1876%e2%80%931965)

Getting up close and personal with Einstein. (2012, March 31). *Jerusalem Post*. Retrieved from http://www.jpost.com/Health-and-Science/Getting-up-close-and-personal-with-Einstein

Hentschel, K. (2011). [Foreword to *Deutsche Physik*; Albert Einstein: Letters to the Prussian Academy of Sciences and the Academy's response (March 28–April 5, 1933)]. In *Physics and National Socialism: An anthology of primary sources*. Basel: Birkhäuser.

Isaacson, W. (2007). *Einstein: His life and universe.* New York: Simon & Schuster.

Philipp Lenard. Retrieved from http://en.wikipedia.org/wiki/Philipp_Lenard

Schirrmacher, A. (2010). *Philipp Lenard: Erinnerungen eines Naturforschers: Kritische annotierte Ausgabe des Originaltyposkriptes von 1931/1943.* Berlin-Heidelberg: Springer Verlag: Berlin-Heidelberg, 2010. (Translation provided by Birgit Ertl-Wagner)

Un-German literature to the bonfire: Nightly Rally by the German Student Union. (1933, May 12). *People's Observer*, North Germany ed. English translation retrieved from www.cyberussr.com/hcunn/volkisch.html

Weissman, G. (2010). X-ray politics: Lenard vs. Roentgen and Einstein. *FASEB Journal, 24,* 1631–1634.

CHAPTER 2: THE HEART OF THE MATTER

Art of Living Blog. Albert Einstein real life stories. Retrieved from http://artoflivingsblog.com/albert-einstein-real-life-stories

Einstein vs. Bohr: How their career long debate led to parallel universes. Retrieved from http://www.imposemagazine.com/bytes/einstein-vs-bohr

Lenard, P. [1927 invitation to the National Socialist Working Party convention, missing its RSVP stub]. Philipp Lenard's bequest, archives of the Deutsches Museum, Munich, Germany, Box NL Lenard 2012-7a.

Schoenbeck, C. (2012). *Albert Einstein und Philipp Lenard: Antipoden im Spannungsfeld von Physik und Zeitgeschichte* (Trans. Brian Stamm). Bayreuth, Germany: Springer.

CHAPTER 3: FAMILIARITY BREEDS CONTEMPT

Einstein, A. (1997). *The collected papers of Albert Einstein* (Vol. 8, Docs. 449 and 562). Princeton, NJ: Princeton University Press.

Einstein, A. (1918, November 29). Dialogue about objections to the theory of relativity (*Dialog über Einwaende gegen die Relativitaetstheorie*; Trans. Wikisource). *Die Naturwissenschaften.* Retrieved from http://en.wikisource.org/wiki/Dialog_about_Objections_against_the_Theory_of_Relativity

Einstein's theory of fidelity. *Telegraph.* Retrieved from http://www.telegraph.co.uk/news/worldnews/northamerica/usa/1523626/Einsteins-theory-of-fidelity.html

Esterson, A. (2007, November). An examination of the revised PBS web pages. Retrieved from http://www.esterson.org/einsteinwife3.htm

Kurzbiographie Eduard Einstein. Retrieved from http://www.einstein-website.de/biographien/einsteineduard.html (Translation provided by Birgit Ertl-Wagner)

Lacayo, R., & Editors of *Time.* (2014). *Albert Einstein: The enduring legacy of a modern genius.* New York: Time.

NBCNews.com. (2006, July 10). New letters shed light on Einstein love life. Retrieved from http://www.nbcnews.com/id/13804030/ns/technology_and_science-science/t/#.U-oAQ0bD8Z8

Philipp Lenard. Retrieved from http://en.wikipedia.org/wiki/Philipp_Lenard

Renn, J., & Schulmann, R. (2001). *Albert Einstein and Mileva Marić: The love letters*. Princeton, NJ: Princeton University Press.

Schirrmacher, A. (2010). *Philipp Lenard: Erinnerungen eines Naturforschers: Kritische annotierte Ausgabe des Originaltyposkriptes von 1931/1943*. Berlin-Heidelberg: Springer. (Translation provided by Birgit Ertl-Wagner)

Schoenbeck, C. (2012). *Albert Einstein und Philipp Lenard: Antipoden im Spannungsfeld von Physik und Zeitgeschichte* (Trans. B. Stamm). Bayreuth, Germany: Springer.

Smith, D. (1996, November 6). Dark side of Einstein emerges in his letters. *New York Times*. Retrieved from http://www.nytimes.com/1996/11/06/arts/dark-side-of-einstein-emerges-in-his-letters.html

Teibel, A. (2006, July 10). Newly unsealed documents throw light on another Einstein lover. *USA Today*. Retrieved from http://usatoday30.usatoday.com/tech/science/discoveries/2006-07-10-einstein-letters-love_x.htm

CHAPTER 4: AN INTERESTING EVENING OUT

Allgemeine Diskussion über die Relativitätstheorie: 86. Naturforscher-Versammlung, Bad Nauheim, 19.-25.9.20. (1920). *Physikalische Zeitschrift, 21* (23/24), 649–699. (Translation provided by Birgit Ertl-Wagner)

Hentschel, K. (2011). [Foreword to *Deutsche Physik*; Albert Einstein: My reply. On the Anti-relativity Theoretical Company, Ltd. (August 27, 1920); Albert Einstein: Letters to the Prussian Academy of Sciences and the Academy's response (March 28–April 5, 1933)]. In *Physics and National Socialism: An anthology of primary sources*. Basel: Birkhäuser.

Kostro, L. (2000). *Einstein and the ether*. Montreal: Apeiron.

Schirrmacher, A. (2010). *Philipp Lenard: Erinnerungen eines Naturforschers: Kritische annotierte Ausgabe des Originaltyposkriptes von 1931/1943*. Berlin: Springer. (Translation provided by Birgit Ertl-Wagner)

Schoenbeck, C. (2012). *Albert Einstein und Philipp Lenard: Antipoden im Spannungsfeld von Physik und Zeitgeschichte* (Trans. B. Stamm). Bayreuth, Germany: Springer.

Van Dongen, J. (2007, June). Reactionaries and Einstein's fame: "German Scientists for the Preservation of Pure Science," relativity, and the Bad Nauheim Meeting. *Physics in Perspective, 9*(2), 212–230. Retrieved from http://arxiv.org/ftp/arxiv/papers/1111/1111.2194.pdf

Weyl, H. (1920). Die Diskussion über die Relativitätstheorie. *Die Umschau, 24*, 609–611 [hardcopy annotated by Philipp Lenard in his own handwriting]. Philipp Lenard's bequest, archives of the Deutsches Museum, Munich, Germany, Box NL Lenard 2012-7b.

CHAPTER 5: A DISAGREEMENT BETWEEN GENTLEMEN

Allgemeine Diskussion über die Relativitätstheorie: 86. Naturforscher-Versammlung, Bad Nauheim, 19.-25.9.20. (1920). *Physikalische Zeitschrift, 21* (23/24), 649–699. (Translation provided by Birgit Ertl-Wagner)

Bad Nauheim. Retrieved from http://en.wikipedia.org/wiki/Bad_Nauheim

Bad Nauheim, Die Gesundheitsstadt. Retrieved from http://www.bad-nauheim.de/tourism.html

Cornwell, J. (2004). Hitler's scientists: Science, war, and the devil's pact. New York: Penguin.

Hentschel, K. (2011). [Foreword to *Deutsche Physik*; Albert Einstein: My reply. On the Anti-relativity Theoretical Company, Ltd. (August 27, 1920); Albert Einstein: Letters to the Prussian Academy of Sciences and the Academy's response (March 28–April 5, 1933)]. In *Physics and National Socialism: An anthology of primary sources*. Basel: Birkhäuser.

Moszkowski Affair. Retrieved from http://www.mathpages.com/home/kmath630/kmath630.htm

Nobelprize.org: The Official Site of the Nobel Prize. Retrieved from http://www.nobelprize.org/nobel_prizes/physics/laureates/

Schirrmacher, A. (2010). *Philipp Lenard: Erinnerungen eines Naturforschers: Kritische annotierte Ausgabe des Originaltyposkriptes von 1931/1943*. Berlin: Springer. (Translation provided by Birgit Ertl-Wagner)

Schoenbeck, C. (2012). *Albert Einstein und Philipp Lenard: Antipoden im Spannungsfeld von Physik und Zeitgeschichte* (Trans. B. Stamm). Bayreuth, Germany: Springer.

Van Dongen, J. (2007, June). Reactionaries and Einstein's fame: "German Scientists for the Preservation of Pure Science," relativity, and the Bad Nauheim Meeting. *Physics in Perspective, 9*(2), 212–230. Retrieved from http://arxiv.org/ftp/arxiv/papers/1111/1111.2194.pdf

Walker, M. (1995). Nazi science: Myth, truth, and the German atomic bomb. Retrieved from http://www.bibliotecapleyades.net/ciencia/nscience/nscience01.htm

CHAPTER 6: A MISSED OPPORTUNITY

Dr. Lewis E. Etter. Retrieved from http://www.findagrave.com/cgi-bin/fg.cgi?page=gr&GRid=62454112

Etter, L. E. (1945). Post-war visit to Roentgen's laboratory. *American Journal of Roentgenology, 54*, 547–552.

Etter, L. E. (1946). Some historical data relating to the discovery of the Roentgen rays. *American Journal of Roentgenology, 56*, 220–231.

Glasser, O. (1934). *Wilhelm Conrad Roentgen and the early history of the X-rays*. Springfield, IL: Charles C. Thomas.

Hillman, B. J., & Goldsmith, J. C. The rise of medical imaging. In *The sorcerer's apprentice: How medical imaging is changing health care*. New York: Oxford University Press.

Lenard, Philipp. (1958). S.v. in *Great men of science*. London: G. Bell and Sons.

Pietzsch, J. (2014). Perspectives: A helping hand from the media. Nobelprize.org: The Official Site of the Nobel Prize. Retrieved from http://www.nobelprize.org/nobel_prizes/physics/laureates/1901/perspectives.html

Roentgen, W. K. (1896). On a New Kind of Rays (*Ueber eine neue Art von Strahlen*). *Nature, 53*, 274–276. Retrieved from http://onlinelibrary.wiley.com/doi/10.3322/canjclin.22.3.153/pdf

von Lenard, P. E. A. (1906, May 28). On cathode rays (Nobel lecture). Nobelprize.org: The Official Site of the Nobel Prize. Retrieved from http://www.nobelprize.org/nobel_prizes/physics/laureates/1905/lenard-lecture.pdf

CHAPTER 7: LENARD IN STOCKHOLM

Alfred Nobel: His life and work. Nobelprize.org: The Official Site of the Nobel Prize. Retrieved from http://www.nobelprize.org/alfred_nobel/biographical/articles/life-work/

Alfred Nobel's will. Nobelprize.org: The Official Site of the Nobel Prize. Retrieved from http://www.nobelprize.org/alfred_nobel/will/

Award ceremony speech. Nobelprize.org: The Official Site of the Nobel Prize. Retrieved from http://www.nobelprize.org/nobel_prizes/physics/laureates/1905/press.html

Banquet menu. Nobelprize.org: The Official Site of the Nobel Prize. Retrieved from http://www.nobelprize.org/ceremonies/menus/

Dress code at the Nobel banquet: What to wear? Nobelprize.org: The Official Site of the Nobel Prize. Retrieved from http://www.nobelprize.org/ceremonies/dresscode/

Early memories of Nobel ceremonies and laureates. Nobelprize.org: The Official Site of the Nobel Prize. Retrieved from http://www.nobelprize.org/ceremonies/eyewitness/morner/index.html

Grandin, K., director of the Royal Swedish Academy of Science Center for the History of Science. Personal communication.

Lenard, P. *Lenard's Faelschungs-Buch* [a red notebook with a handwritten title in red pencil on the first page, "Faelschungs-Buch (Autobiogr. wichtig)]. Philipp Lenard's bequest, archives of the Deutsches Museum, Munich, Germany, Folder 3 NL Lenard 2012.

Nobel banquet. Nobelprize.org: The Official Site of the Nobel Prize. Retrieved from http://en.wikipedia.org/wiki/Nobel_Prize#Nobel_banquet

Prize amount and market value of invested capital converted into 2013 year's monetary value. Nobelprize.org: The Official Site of the Nobel Prize. Retrieved from http://www.nobelprize.org/nobel_prizes/about/amounts/prize_amounts_14.pdf

Schirrmacher, A. (2010). *Philipp Lenard: Erinnerungen eines Naturforschers: Kritische annotierte Ausgabe des Originaltyposkriptes von 1931/1943*. Berlin-Heidelberg: Springer Verlag: Berlin-Heidelberg, 2010. (Translation provided by Birgit Ertl-Wagner)

von Lenard, P. E. A. (1906, May 28). On cathode rays (Nobel lecture). Nobelprize.org: The Official Site of the Nobel Prize. Retrieved from http://www.nobelprize.org/nobel_prizes/physics/laureates/1905/lenard-lecture.pdf

CHAPTER 8: EINSTEIN VERSUS THE SMALL POPES OF UPPSALA

Award ceremony speech. Nobelprize.org: The Official Site of the Nobel Prize. Retrieved from http://www.nobelprize.org/nobel_prizes/physics/laureates/1921/press.html

Clark, S. (2012, October 8). Why Einstein never received a Nobel Prize for relativity. Nobelprize.org: The Official Site of the Nobel Prize. Retrieved from http://www.theguardian.com/science/across-the-universe/2012/oct/08/einstein-nobel-prize-relativity

Einstein, A. (1920). *Relativity: The special and general theory*. New York: Henry Holt.

Elzinga, A. (2006). *Einstein's Nobel Prize: A glimpse behind closed doors*. Sagamore Beach, NY: Science History.

Explore 100 famous scientist quotes. Retrieved from http://www.todayinsci.com/QuotationsCategories/N_Cat/NobelPrize-Quotations.htm

Friedman, R. M. (2001). Einstein must never get a Nobel Prize: Keeping physics safe for Sweden. In *The politics of excellence: Behind the Nobel Prize in Science* (Chap. 7). New York: Henry Holt.

Fundamental ideas and problems with the theory of relativity. Retrieved from http://www.nobelprize.org/nobel_prizes/physics/laureates/1921/einstein-lecture.html

Grandin, K., director of the Royal Swedish Academy of Science Center for the History of Science. Personal communication. Letter from Philipp Lenard complaining about Albert Einstein being awarded the Nobel Prize.

Hughs, V. (2006, September). Einstein vs. the Nobel Prize: Why the Nobel Committee repeatedly dissed this "world-bluffing Jewish physicist." *Discover*. Retrieved from http://discovermagazine.com/2006/sep/einstein-nobel-prize/

CHAPTER 9: DANGEROUS CHOICES
AND CHAPTER 10: LENARD AND HITLER

Ash, M. G., & Sollner, A. (1996). *Forced migration and scientific change: Émigré German-speaking scientists and scholars after 1933*. Berlin: German Historical Institute.

Beer hall putsch. Retrieved from http://www.historyplace.com/worldwar2/timeline/putsch2.htm

Cornwell, J. (2004). *Hitler's scientists: Science, war, and the devil's pact*. New York: Penguin.

Erwin Schroedinger. Retrieved from http://www.nobelprize.org/nobel_prizes/physics/laureates/1933/schrodinger-bio.html

Gustav von Kahr. Retrieved from http://de.wikipedia.org/wiki/Gustav_von_Kahr

Hentschel, K. (2011). [The Hitler Spirit and Science; Max von Laue's review of Johannes Stark's "The current crisis in German physics"; Albert von Brunn's review of "100 authors against Hitler"]. In *Physics and National Socialism: An anthology of primary sources*. Basel: Birkhäuser.

Hitler, A. [Letters to Philipp Lenard]. Philipp Lenard's bequest, archives of the Deutsches Museum, Munich, Germany, Box NL Lenard 2012-7a.

Hitler speech on Enabling Act 1933: Complete text: The last day of the Weimar Republic. Retrieved from http://worldfuturefund.org/Reports2013/hitlerenablingact.htm

The law that enabled Hitler's dictatorship. Retrieved from http://www.dw.de/the-law-that-enabled-hitlers-dictatorship/a-16689839

Lenard, P. [Transcription by Mr. Pleissen of a speech given by Lenard in Heidelberg, spring 1922, sent to Philipp Lenard's Heidelberg address on November 9, 1936]. Philipp Lenard's bequest, archives of the Deutsches Museum, Munich, Germany, Folder 3 NL Lenard 2012

Lenard, P. *Lenard's Faelschungs-Buch* [a red notebook with a handwritten title in red pencil on the first page, "Faelschungs-Buch (Autobiogr. wichtig)]. Philipp Lenard's bequest, archives of the Deutsches Museum, Munich, Germany, Folder 3 NL Lenard 2012.

Loewenstein, A. Pragmatic and dogmatic physics: Anti-Semitism in *Nature*, 1938. Retrieved from http://www.relativitycalculator.com/pdfs/critique_nature_magazine.pdf

Morris, D. G. (2005). *Justice imperiled; The anti-Nazi lawyer Max Hirschberg in Weimar Germany*. Ann Arbor: University of Michigan Press.

Physik und Politik. (1922, June 30). *Neue Zürcher Zeitung*, (860). (Translation provided by Birgit Ertl-Wagner)

Religious views of Adolf Hitler. Retrieved from http://en.wikiquote.org/wiki/Adolf_Hitler%27s_religious_views

Schoenbeck, C. (2012). *Albert Einstein und Philipp Lenard: Antipoden im Spannungsfeld von Physik und Zeitgeschichte* (Trans. Brian Stamm). Bayreuth, Germany: Springer.

Walker, M. (1995). Nazi science: Myth, truth, and the German atomic bomb. Retrieved from http://www.bibliotecapleyades.net/ciencia/nscience/nscience01.htm

CHAPTER 11: *DEUTSCHE PHYSIK*

Albert Einstein: Pacifism and Zionism. Retrieved from http://www.sparknotes.com/biography/einstein/section8.rhtml

Hentschel, K. (2011). [Foreword to *Deutsche Physik*; Organization of Physical Research; A big day for science: Johannes Stark appointed president of the PTR. In *Physics and National Socialism: An anthology of primary sources*. Basel: Birkhäuser.

Manifesto of the 93 German Intellectuals. Retrieved from http://wwi.lib.byu.edu/index.php/Manifesto_of_the_Ninety-Three_German_Intellectuals

Max Planck. Retrieved from http://www.sparknotes.com/biography/planck/section5.rhtml

The Rape of Belgium. Retrieved from http://en.wikipedia.org/wiki/The_Rape_of_Belgium

Walker, M. (1995). Nazi science: Myth, truth, and the German atomic bomb. Retrieved from http://www.bibliotecapleyades.net/ciencia/nscience/nscience01.htm

Wolff, S. L. (2003). Physicists in the "Krieg der Geister": Wilhelm Wien's "Proclamation." *Historical Studies in the Physical and Biological Sciences, 33*(2), 337–368.

Wolff, S. L. (2006). Die Ausgrenzung und Vertreibung von Physikern im Nationalsozialismus—welche Rolle spielte die DPG? In D. Hoffmann & M. Walker (Eds.), *Physiker zwischen Autonomie und Anpassung* (pp. 91–138). Weinheim, Germany: Wiley-VCH.

CHAPTER 12: ACADEMIC IMPURITIES

Albert Einstein. Retrieved from http://www.princetonhistory.org/collections/albert-einstein.cfm

Anti-Jewish legislation in pre-war Germany. Retrieved from http://www.ushmm.org/wlc/en/article.php?ModuleId=10005681

Ash, M. G., & Sollner, A. (1996). *Forced migration and scientific change: Émigré German-speaking scientists and scholars after 1933*. Berlin: German Historical Institute.

Bentwich, N. (1953). *Rescue and achievement of refugee scholars*. The Hague: Martinus Nijhoff.

Beyerchen, A. D. (1980). *Wissenschaftler unter Hitler*. Cologne: Kiepenheuer & Witsch. (Translation provided by Birgit Ertl-Wagner)

The Born Einstein Letters. Retrieved from http://archive.org/stream/TheBornEinsteinLetters/Born-TheBornEinsteinLetters_djvu.txt

Der "Vater der Wasserstoffbombe" ist tot. Retrieved from http://www.sueddeutsche.de/politik/edward-teller-der-vater-der-wasserstoffbombe-ist-tot-1.931841

Edward Teller. Retrieved from http://www.spiegel.de/spiegel/print/d-28591090.html

Edward Teller. Retrieved from http://de.wikipedia.org/wiki/Edward_Teller

Edward Teller. Retrieved from http://education.llnl.gov/archives/edward-teller#1

Edward Teller. Retrieved from http://en.wikiquote.org/wiki/Edward_Teller

Fritz Haber. Retrieved from http://en.wikipedia.org/wiki/Fritz_Haber

Hentschel, K. (2011). [Introduction; Law for the Restoration of the Professional Civil Service; First Ordinance on the Implementation of the Law for the Restoration of the Professional Civil Service; Fritz Haber's letter of resignation to Minister Rust; Johannes Stark's personal evaluations of G. Hertz and R. Gans for the German University Lecturers Association; Goettingen University lecturers; Professor Franck's resignation; W. Heisenberg's letter to Max Born; My Audience with Adolf Hitler]. In *Physics and National Socialism: An anthology of primary sources*. Basel: Birkhäuser.

Ivry, B. (2011, November 25). The man who outsainted Einstein [James Franck material]. *Jewish Daily Forward*. Retrieved from http://forward.com/articles/146281/the-man-who-out-sainted-einstein/

James Franck. Retrieved from http://www.aip.org/history/acap/biographies/bio.jsp?franckj

James Franck. Retrieved from http://de.wikipedia.org/wiki/James_Franck

James Franck, Letter of resignation to the rector of the Georg-August University in Goettingen. Retrieved from https://www.uni-goettingen.de/de/brief-von-james-franck-an-den-rektor-der-georg-august-universitaet-vom-17-april-1933/85743.html (Translation provided by Birgit Ertl-Wagner)

Max Born. Retrieved from http://en.wikipedia.org/wiki/Max_Born

Obituary of James Franck. Retrieved from http://de.wikipedia.org/wiki/Datei:Nachruf_Franck_1964_G%C3%B6ttingen.jpg

Reich Chancellery. Retrieved from http://en.wikipedia.org/wiki/Reich_Chancellery

Teller vs. Pauling. Retrieved from http://scarc.library.oregonstate.edu/coll/pauling/peace/video/1958v.3.html

Walker, M. (1995). Nazi science: Myth, truth, and the German atomic bomb. Retrieved from http://www.bibliotecapleyades.net/ciencia/nscience/nscience01.htm

CHAPTER 13: SOME SAY BY FIRE, OTHERS ICE

Cornwell, J. (2004). *Hitler's scientists: Science, war, and the devil's pact*. New York: Penguin Books.

Goudsmit, S. A. (1986). *Alsos*. New York: Tomash.

Heinrich Himmler. Retrieved from http://www.newworldencyclopedia.org/entry/Heinrich_Himmler

Hentschel, K. (2011). [Introduction; W. Menzel: German physics and Jewish physics; W. Heisenberg: On the article "German physics and Jewish physics"; Das Schwarze Korps white Jews in science; J. Stark comment on W. Heisenberg's reply; J. Stark: Science is politically bankrupt; Heinrich Himmler letter to Werner Heisenberg]. In *Physics and National Socialism: An anthology of primary sources*. Basel: Birkhäuser.

Himmler: A mommy's boy monster. Retrieved from http://www.express.co.uk/expressyourself/284679/Himmler-A-mummy-s-boy-monster

Holton, G. Werner Heisenberg and Albert Einstein. Retrieved from http://www-personal.umich.edu/~samuels/214/other/news/Holton.html

Walker, M. (1995). Nazi science: Myth, truth, and the German atomic bomb. Retrieved from http://www.bibliotecapleyades.net/ciencia/nscience/nscience01.htm

Werner Heisenberg. Retrieved from http://www.informationphilosopher.com/solutions/scientists/heisenberg

Werner Heisenberg. Retrieved from http://www.fampeople.com/cat-werner-heisenberg_6

EPILOGUE

Albert Einstein. Retrieved from http://www.cssforum.com.pk/off-topic-section/general-knowledge-quizzes-iq-tests/6849-albert-einstein.html

Dr. Albert Einstein dies in sleep at 76; world mourns loss of great scientist. Retrieved from http://www.nytimes.com/learning/general/onthisday/bday/0314.html

Lacayo, R., & Editors of *Time*. (2014). *Albert Einstein: The enduring legacy of a modern genius*. New York: Time.

Letter from Albert Einstein to FDR, 8/2/39. Retrieved from http://www.pbs.org/wgbh/americanexperience/features/primary-resources/truman-ein39/

Einstein to Roosevelt, August 2, 1939. Retrieved from http://www.dannen.com/ae-fdr.html

Johanna Fantova. Retrieved from http://www.menscheinstein.de/biografie/biografie_jsp/key=3166.html (Translation provided by Birgit Ertl-Wagner)

Letters from alums about Albert Einstein in Princeton Alumni Weekly. Retrieved from http://www.princeton.edu/paw/web_exclusives/more/more_letters/letters_einstein

Schirrmacher, A. (2010). *Philipp Lenard: Erinnerungen eines Naturforschers: Kritische annotierte Ausgabe des Originaltyposkriptes von 1931/1943*. Berlin: Springer. (Translation provided by Birgit Ertl-Wagner)

ACKNOWLEDGMENTS

The authors are pleased to thank a number of individuals who made important contributions to *The Man Who Stalked Einstein*.

Foremost among these is Pam Wexler Hillman, who listened to her husband read the entire book aloud, chapter by chapter, sometimes more than once, before turning out the lights at night. Her comments helped identify ambiguous and hard-to-understand passages and improved the quality of the writing.

None of us had ever had an agent for anything, but serendipity led us to a great one. Claire Gerus believed in the project from the beginning, encouraged us, advised us through the writing process, and continues to serve our interests in this and future projects.

We were assigned a wonderful editor, lost him following a buyout of our initial publisher, and found him again. Jon Sternfeld's vision matched our own. Perhaps more important, he has a remarkable knack for simultaneously encouraging our best work while pointing out how something could be improved. Absent Jon's efforts, this book would be a lesser work.

We are grateful for the efforts on our behalf of Ronald Coleman and his colleagues at the library of the U.S. Holocaust Memorial Museum for their assistance in getting us started on the research that eventually led to this book.

Professors Hans Ringertz and Per Carlson helped us to connect with Professor Karl Grandin, director of the Royal Swedish Academy of Science Center for the History of Science, who provided us with background on Philipp Lenard's Nobel Prize and shared Lenard's letter to the Academy disputing Einstein's selection for the 1921 Nobel Prize.

Dr. Alan Matsumoto, chair of the Department of Radiology and Medical Imaging at the University of Virginia, encouraged the writing of this book and supported the endeavor.

Dr. Wilhelm Fuessl, head of the archives of the Deutsches Museum in Munich, granted us access to archived boxes of Lenard's personal documents and laboratory books. Some of this material found its way into these pages. Brian Stamm translated into English a critical journal article by Charlotte Schoenbeck, "Albert Einstein und Philipp Lenard: Antipoden im Spannungsfeld von Physik und Zeitgeschichte."

Finally, we thank the Charlottesville, Virginia, writing critique group to which Bruce belonged for a number of years—Sharon Hostler, Susan Guerrant, Gerry Kruger, Marian Dewalt, Peggy Brown, Sharon Davies, and Linn Harrison—who did their best to help him learn to write.

INDEX

ABOUT THE AUTHORS

Bruce J. Hillman, MD, has distinguished himself as a health services researcher, clinical trialist, and author of both medical articles and short stories published in elite magazines and journals. He is professor and former chair of radiology at the University of Virginia School of Medicine. He has published over 300 medical articles, book chapters, and editorials, including his 2010 book for the lay public, *The Sorcerer's Apprentice: How Medical Imaging Is Changing Health Care* (Oxford University Press). Dr. Hillman has served as editor-in-chief of three medical journals, including his current position with the *Journal of the American College of Radiology*. He was deputy editor of the online literary and humanities journal *Hospital Drive*, and has published eight short stories in such journals as *The Connecticut Review*, *Compass Rose*, and *Aethlon, the Journal of Sports Literature*.

Birgit Ertl-Wagner, MD, MHBA, is professor of magnetic resonance imaging at the Ludwig-Maximilian University and a neuroradiologist at the Grosshadern university hospital in Munich, Germany. Her research focus lies in the realm of neuroscience with an emphasis on functional neuroimaging. She has authored or coauthored over 130 original articles, review articles, and book chapters. She has also written five textbooks in German (four on radiological topics and one on quality management), all of which are in their second editions. Dr. Ertl-Wagner is married to the historian Bernd C. Wagner. They live in Munich, Germany, with their three children. Their family conversations often focus on the intersections of medicine, technology, and the humanities.

Bernd C. Wagner, PhD, is a senior manager in the IT service industry following a successful career in consulting and corporate strategy. He studied history and philosophy in Munich, Germany, and Edinburgh, UK, and the University of Bochum, Germany, where he wrote his thesis on the topic "IG Auschwitz." He authored a book based on his thesis detailing the involvement of German industry in the genocide conducted at Auschwitz, and he was coeditor of two books on related topics.

AVON PUBLIC LIBRARY
BOX 977 / 200 BENCHMARK RD
AVON, COLORADO 81620